HISTORY OF THE THOROUGHGOOD NEIGHBORHOOD

(1955 to 2013)

THOROUGHGOOD CIVIC LEAGUE,
PAM SPILLMAN, HISTORIAN

outskirtspress
DENVER, COLORADO

The opinions expressed in this manuscript are solely the opinions of the author and do not represent the opinions or thoughts of the publisher. The author has represented and warranted full ownership and/or legal right to publish all the materials in this book.

History of the Thoroughgood Neighborhood
(1955 to 2013)
All Rights Reserved.
Copyright © 2013 Thoroughgood Civic League
v3.0

Cover image by Timothy Hanna. Copied with permission of Mark A. Reed, Historic Resources Coordinator, City of Virginia Beach, Virginia. U. S.

This book may not be reproduced, transmitted, or stored in whole or in part by any means, including graphic, electronic, or mechanical without the express written consent of the publisher except in the case of brief quotations embodied in critical articles and reviews.

Outskirts Press, Inc.
http://www.outskirtspress.com

ISBN: 978-1-4787-0265-8

U.S. Copyright Number: TXu 1-853-150

Outskirts Press and the "OP" logo are trademarks belonging to Outskirts Press, Inc.

PRINTED IN THE UNITED STATES OF AMERICA

Table of Contents

Preface v
Acknowledgements vii
Foreword ix
Chapter 1 – The Beginning 1
Chapter 2 – Neighborhood Anchors 31
Chapter 3 – The Sixties 53
Chapter 4 – The Seventies 69
Chapter 5 – The Eighties 79
Chapter 6 – The Nineties 99
Chapter 7 – 2000 to 2013 113
Chapter 8 – Who's Who 131
Appendix A – Timeline 143
Appendix B – Former TCL Presidents 149
Appendix C – Membership/Dues Trends 163

Preface

Thoroughgood is a well-known, respected neighborhood in Hampton Roads. Thanks to the early development efforts of the Collier family, it was one of the first large-scale, luxury sub-divisions in the City of Virginia Beach. The majority of lot sizes were expansive, and the homes spacious and elegant, especially for the times. It was THE place to live in Virginia Beach.

Unlike many new developments going up today, every effort was made to save the trees and maintain a woodland, rural feel. It was a pleasure to enter through the gates of Thoroughgood. In the spring, Thoroughgood yards rivaled Norfolk's Azalea Gardens for the dazzling display of mature azaleas on display. In the dog days of summer, the temperature seemed to drop a couple of degrees under the canopy of trees. And while fall meant lots of leaf raking for its residents, the colors were vibrant and awe-inspiring. Parents felt comforted knowing their children would attend both elementary and middle school years nestled within the safe bounds of the large neighborhood – away from the hustle-bustle of large roads and busy intersections. And, residents were proud to live amongst such esteemed history.

Despite all the positives, a neighborhood doesn't always stay as it starts out without the care, guidance, and hard work of dedicated concerned citizens. First, the pride of the majority of our residents is evident as they toil extensively to maintain, update and "showcase" their properties. Next, Thoroughgood Civic League has given much of their time and talents over the years to meet and solve each property challenge presented, ensuring that this neighborhood continued to grow and prosper. In fact, the neighborhood would look much different today had the Civic League not been as engaged as it was. Thoroughgood and Hermitage Garden Clubs have been willing partners to ensure the yards and entrances are the most beautiful in the city. And Thoroughgood Elementary and Independence Middle Schools, in partnership with a strong and active PTA and loving, engaged parents, provided an excellent foundation for generation after generation of children who grow up to prosper and do great things in the world.

This neighborhood has seen tremendous change and overcome significant obstacles in its fifty-plus years of existence. Through this book, Thoroughgood Civic League has attempted to tell our story. Although every effort was made to ensure the information is correct, we relied on Civic League records and memories of longtime residents. Formal research sources (city hall, libraries and newspapers) were used extensively for information as available from a relatively new city. We hope you enjoy reading it as much as we enjoyed researching and writing it. Even our long time residents might learn something new about this wonderful community.

Acknowledgements

For his broad Princess Anne County perspective and historical research advice, special thanks is offered to Dr. Stephen Mansfield, professor at Virginia Wesleyan College and author of the wonderful book, "Princess Anne County and Virginia Beach...a pictorial history." That book and the subsequent interview with Dr. Mansfield formed the starting point for this book.

Also appreciated were the advice, counsel and interest shown by Bob Perrine, who wrote the very interesting "Old Donation History."

Next, thanks are due to the many Thoroughgood homeowners that were willing to be interviewed and generously shared their memories and recollections for this written history, including:

- Anne Greenberg, Howard and Suzanne Horton, and Sue McGeorge who together made Ewell Point "come alive" in its very interesting and long history;
- Joyce Barry, spouse of a prior Thoroughgood Civic League president, who enthusiastically gave a wealth of information regarding the Thoroughgood and Hermitage Garden Clubs and shared her infectious love of history;
- Andy Mullen who made Hermitage Point sound positively irresistible;
- Starr Plimpton, spouse and daughter-in-law of prior Thoroughgood Civic League presidents, who for years took such good care of our namesake Adam Thoroughgood House and continues her support of it today;
- Frank and Lois Wootton who did so many things behind the scenes to maintain zoning standards;

- George Stenke who has long cared for our earth dam and nearby Lake Charles, and who generously advanced funds to finance the original publishing of this book;
- Marianne Littel who, along with her husband has taken excellent care of the "other" historic home in our neighborhood – The Hermitage House;
- (The incomparable) Earnestine Middleton whose energy for civic duty is awe-inspiring;
- Ben Owen, longtime resident of and wealth of information about Country Club Circle;
- Kent "Curly" Weber, prior Thoroughgood Civic League president who was truly a stalwart entity for Thoroughgood Civic League Board for so many years;
- Laura Bruno, who was the former Historian (and might have been the first Historian as well!) for the Thoroughgood Civic League;
- Susan Atkins, spouse of a prior Thoroughgood Civic League president, who works hard to publish our very informative newsletters – "Thoroughly Good News;"
- Tania and Tom Farley, who along with Susan Atkins enthusiastically assisted in proofreading, and formed the committee to plan the publishing of this history;
- Mark Reed (Historic Resources Coordinator for the City of Virginia Beach, Department of Museums), who provided permission to use the Tim Hanna drawing of the Adam Thoroughgood House, as depicted on the front cover;
- My son Matthew Horner, who after years of being the recipient of my critiquing his school-age writing has himself turned into quite a good editor and I thank him for his editing of this book;
- A special thanks to my mentors (and proofreaders!) Clyde March and Bob Coffey. Bob and Clyde (both prior Thoroughgood Civic League Presidents) have a long distinguished history of civic leadership to, and care deeply about our neighborhood. Both provided a bevy of much needed contacts and information for this book. They also offered continuous support, advice and counsel;
- Finally, I would like to thank my husband Ed, who graciously put our retirement on hold while this history was being written. His patience, support and encouragement were my greatest strengths.

Foreword
by Dr. Stephen Mansfield

After two and a half centuries as a sparsely populated rural county, with less than 20,000 residents at the beginning of World War II, Princess Anne experienced dramatic post-war growth during the 1950s, reflected in the emergence of Thoroughgood and other communities that accommodated the influx of population. As Pam Spillman has documented here in HISTORY OF THE THOROUGHGOOD NEIGHBORHOOD, 1955-2013, this community in some ways parallels the saga of other neighborhoods while remaining distinctive in key respects.

James N. Collier died very soon after his 1955 purchase of the acreage which comprised the first phase of Thoroughgood, but his dream of a neighborhood of expansive, wooded lots within a pastoral setting was embraced by his sons, the Thorogood Corporation, and the civic league which was organized as the first residents arrived. To maintain the quality of life they valued, residents used their collective will to monitor changes in issues such as public services, school boundaries, and zoning decisions; the author observes, "Thoroughgood has always had the reputation of being a formidable opponent to Beach government."

In addition to remaining highly desirable as a residential community with a rural flavor, Thoroughgood is distinctive as the site of the historic Adam Thoroughgood House. The presence of the house ties the community to the area of earliest permanent English settlement in what is now Virginia Beach, and the author's detective work links Collier's choice of street names to many of the settlers brought to the Virginia colony by the first Adam Thoroughgood under the head rights system.

Readers beyond the Thoroughgood neighborhood will appreciate references to when house numbers, zip codes, sanitary sewers, telephone exchanges, neighborhood watches and other developments became part of life. In this and other respects all Virginia Beach residents will find the book helpful. As the modern city of Virginia Beach and many of its older neighborhoods reach the half-century mark and beyond, young families increasingly are succeeding first generation homeowners, and the institutional memory of founding generations is fading, it is important for every neighborhood to create a written history of its community. This well-researched, comprehensive, and engaging Thoroughgood story will serve as an intriguing and beneficial resource for those persons who call Thoroughgood home but also as a model well worth emulating by other neighborhoods.

CHAPTER 1

The Beginning

Introduction. Long before the Thoroughgood neighborhood was developed, the name of our neighborhood had been established upon the arrival of Adam Thoroughgood in 1622. He was considered to be Virginia Beach's first settler, according to a 1998 special edition of the Beacon to commemorate the founding of Virginia Beach. In "An Economic and Social Survey of Princess Anne County," by E. E. Ferebee and J. Pendleton Wilson, Jr., Adam Thoroughgood was described as one of the most prominent, if not *the* most prominent man in Princess Anne County. From his humble beginnings as an indentured servant, Adam Thoroughgood became a large landowner, a Justice of the Court, and a member of the Governor's Council. The Thoroughgood neighborhood we live in today was carved out of a piece of Adam Thoroughgood's original Grand Patent. It is the palpable history in the soil under our feet that makes this neighborhood so very special.

A Community Older than its City. When Thoroughgood was originally developed in the late 1950s, the area it inhabited was in Princess Anne County – not yet Virginia Beach. According to *"1607 – 2007: 400 Facts About Princess Anne County and Virginia Beach History,"* Virginia Beach was incorporated as a town in 1906, and as a city in 1952. However, the "city" in 1952 consisted of merely the two-mile resort area. It wasn't until 1963 that Princess Anne County merged with this two-mile resort area to form the City of Virginia Beach most of us are familiar with today. For most of its history, Princess Anne County was rural and agricultural. In "Lower Tidewater Virginia" Volume 2, Rogers Dey Wichard, Ph.D. explained Norfolk was growing at such a rapid pace it created a giant demand for housing.

◄ HISTORY OF THE THOROUGHGOOD NEIGHBORHOOD

As Virginia Beach grew into a popular resort town and transportation from Norfolk to Virginia Beach improved, Norfolk residents were attracted to the pleasant lands around the Lynnhaven River. In addition, Navy presence at Little Creek and Oceana, and Army presence at Fort Story drew people to Princess Anne County. An article in the Virginian Pilot (July 9, 2012) said this sprawling suburban city (i.e., Virginia Beach) burst into existence in the 1960s as droves of suburbanites fled nearby Norfolk and Portsmouth in pursuit of a simpler lifestyle – bigger yards, less crime, and lower taxes.

As development continued, farmland diminished. Dr. Wichard reported Princess Anne County had 1,432 farms in 1900 and 1,180 farms in 1930. By 1958 it was down to 692 farms. A special edition of the Beacon commemorating the 35th anniversary of Virginia Beach in 1998 noted the number of farms in Virginia Beach in 1992 had reduced to 156.

Development of the Original Thoroughgood. This chapter will concentrate on the original (and largest) section of Thoroughgood as developed in the 1950s. According to an article in the Virginia Beach/Beacon (November 14, 1998), land for the original Thoroughgood neighborhood was purchased by James N. Collier, President of Thorogood Corporation. *(Note: According to an article in the Virginian Pilot/Beacon November 14, 1998), the "Thorogood" spelling resulted from variations of the family name found in records. For consistency sake, it will be spelled as "Thorogood" when referring to the corporation.)* The land was comprised of 500+ acres of Princess Anne County farmland, procured in three main transactions. Deed Book and page references are provided in case the reader would like to do further research on the property at the Virginia Beach Courthouse.

- Approximately 236 acres came from Greenbrier Farm on February 28, 1955 (Deed Book 394, page 459). The deed from Greenbrier Farms to Thorogood Corporation says the purchase included "all furniture and equipment located in the old Thoroughgood brick house." But there is also a separate deed of purchase of the Adam Thoroughgood House from Thorrowgood Manor, Inc. to Thorogood Corporation also on February 28, 1955 (Deed Book 394, page 463). It is unclear as to the differences in the two deeds, but a Virginian Pilot story (December 23, 1954) said the Thrasher family of Greenbrier Farms represented the principals of Thorrowgood Manor, Inc. and the entire sale consisted of the Thoroughgood House and about

THE BEGINNING

236 acres for a consideration reported to be $225,000. The newspaper article interviewed James Collier who mentioned a "number of adventurous individuals" he had encountered around the Adam Thoroughgood House who were using metal detectors to search for "pirate" treasure. The hunt was likely related to the fact that nearby Bay Lake Pines was reputed to have been one of Blackbeard the Pirate's favorite resting places.

- The largest tract (313.9 acres of land and 18.15 acres of oyster coves) was purchased from Ferrell and Linda Moore on April 9, 1955 (Deed Book 399, page 30). The deed provides much historical reference itself. It says the Ferrell Moore property was formerly known as the "Thompson or Murphy Farm," and later known as "Bayside Farm," and at the time of purchase was known as "Hermitage." The deed further said lands formerly owned by George Garrison and later owned by Grace M. Keeler, and currently owned by the grantee bound the land on the north. The deed said the south of the Ferrell property purchase was bounded by the lands of A. E. Ewell and C. C. Frizzell.
- The final piece of property purchased by the Thorogood Corporation was for the front entrance of Thoroughgood (about 2 acres). This property was purchased from the School Board of Princess Anne County on July 15, 1955 (Deed Book 411, page 544). For those curious as to why the School Board would have previously owned the entrance, see the paragraph on the old fireplace further down in this chapter.

The neighborhood boundaries of these 500+ acres were Pleasure House Road to the west, Bayville Farms (i.e., Church Point) to the north, and Lynnhaven River to the east. The southern boundary of the property was a string of roads – Hermitage Road, Reynolds Drive, Dunstan Lane (just the part that would be in front of Thoroughgood Elementary School), and the north side of Ewell Road as far as Stanfield Road.

Although those 500+ acres comprised the original part of Thoroughgood, Thorogood Corporation did not develop *the entire* Thoroughgood neighborhood as we know it today. At the time of the purchase, there were farms surrounding the original tract purchased by the Colliers – World's End Farm which was developed into Ewell Point; White Acre Farm near what would become Independence

HISTORY OF THE THOROUGHGOOD NEIGHBORHOOD

Middle School and White Acre Road and Court; Oliver Farm that later became Thoroughgood Colony; and, Frizzell Farm, which formed the early part of Thoroughgood Estates. These and other sections on Delray Drive, Blackthorne Court, Wakefield Court, were developed by others. Chapters 3 through 7 will discuss the expansion of Thoroughgood beyond the original boundaries in follow-on decades, and the other developers.

At the time of original development however, neither Thoroughgood Elementary School nor Independence Middle Schools were built. The main entrance off Pleasure House Road was mostly wooded, with the exception of the sales office at the end of Thoroughgood Square (now home to the Virginia Independent Automobile Dealer's Association). Home sites did not begin until after Collier Lane. Large brick columns were built to announce the entrance on either side of Thoroughgood Square. According to longtime resident Andy Mullen, the columns were flanked on their outer boundaries by a long wooden fence. Mr. Mullen said it was a four rail (not split rail fence) that resembled something that might have been found in a wealthy country estate. He also said that the street signs were unique – a carved white post, white sign surrounded with wrought iron scrollwork. The road names were done with black lettering. There were no home sites in the end of Country Club Circle nearest the Adam Thoroughgood House. This section was originally planned as a Country Club. The original neighborhood proudly had no curbs, gutters, or sidewalks, something that has been preferred and fought for over the years in an effort to maintain that "rural" feeling as described in an article about the neighborhood in the Virginian Pilot/Beacon (November 14, 1998).

Some of the home sites were built on property fronting the Lynnhaven River, Thoroughgood Cove, and Lake Charles. Lake Charles was built as a private lake. The lake, according to a Virginian Pilot/Beacon article (May 18, 1967) was originally marshy land that was dammed up and dredged out to form a lake. The dam still remains to preserve Lake Charles, and serves to connect Moores Lane (off Hermitage Road) to Swan Lake Drive (off Country Club Circle). Some of our longtime residents recall driving an automobile across the dam, or fishing from the dam. Both Moores Lane and Swan Lake Drive are privately owned, and according to the Beacon article, the lake is also private since each home site bordering it extends to the center of the lake. This is also how it looks on the original composite plat since the body of water for Lake

THE BEGINNING

Charles does not appear as an open lake. Instead it appears that the home site property lines extend into the center of the lake.

There was no city sewer for Thoroughgood until the late 1970s – homes used septic tanks. The Civic League pursued sewer lines early and vigorously, but their installation was pending completion of the Little Creek Sewer Plant, as well as sufficient funds for construction from fledgling newborn city coffers. City water was not available to all residents until the late 1960s. Before that residents relied on wells. And natural gas wasn't even on the neighborhood's early wish list.

Transfer and Restoration of Adam Thoroughgood House. Right after the purchase of the land, James Collier sought to preserve and restore the Adam Thoroughgood House, so he sold the house and surrounding 2.29 acres to the Adam Thoroughgood Foundation on August 31, 1955 (Deed Book 418, page 596). The sales price is unclear: the deed says the sale was for $10.00, but several newspaper articles at the time reported the sale at $25,000. Regardless of the price, Mr. Collier would later generously donate to the restoration of the house. The boundaries of the Adam Thoroughgood House sale went from Country Club Circle to the south, and Parish Road to the west, similar to today. However, the property east of the house only had a small "finger" that reached the Lynnhaven River. Gladys D. Pearson owned most of the present day backyard then. See Chapter 7 for how that property was later procured for the Adam Thoroughgood House.

The north side of the Thoroughgood House property did not reach Thoroughgood Drive at the time – it instead stopped at Lot 299 of the original Thoroughgood community plat. In 1956, James Collier conveyed Lot 299 to the Adam Thoroughgood House Foundation (Deed Book 473, page 544).

Henry C. Hofheimer, II was the president of the Adam Thoroughgood House Foundation. James Collier was on the Board of Directors for the Foundation, and also provided a monetary donation to help with the preservation costs – $15,000 according to newspaper reports. According to the book "Lower Tidewater Virginia," the restoration was under the direction of Finlay F. Ferguson, formerly associated with Colonial Williamsburg. A goal of $115,000 in fund-raising was sought for the renovation. According to "Historic Preservation," the quarterly of the National Trust for Historic Preservation (Spring 1955), the National Trust had been working with the foundation in an advisory capacity. The Natural Trust reported that restoration plans called for

◄ HISTORY OF THE THOROUGHGOOD NEIGHBORHOOD

an intensive archaeological and historical investigation followed by restoration of the house under a Board of nationally recognized experts. The restoration was scheduled to be through its major phase in time for the 350th anniversary of the founding of Jamestown in 1957. In addition, Mr. Hofheimer traveled all over Europe to furnish the house spending an estimated $250,000 for period furniture and decorations. The house was dedicated to the Foundation and was made a museum open to the public in a ceremony held April 29, 1957, just two weeks before James Collier's untimely death - more about Mr. Collier in Chapter 2.

Detailed Plat Information - Sections of Original Thoroughgood. There were eight eventual sections of Thoroughgood, not including Thoroughgood Estates. Sections 1-6 are described below. These were the plats developed in the late 1950s, and were all developed by the Colliers. The other sections will be discussed in the chapter for the decade in which they were developed. For the curious, the date of the plat, map book, and page of the map book are provided in case the reader would like to look up the plat at the Virginia Beach Municipal Center, County Clerk's Office, Building 10B, 3rd floor. Note that the page numbers provided are correct for using hard copy maps. If using computerized maps, the page may be off slightly.

- Section 1 (July 1955, Map Book 39, page 37-41) is the original "backside" of Thoroughgood bounded by Five Forks Road, Two Woods Road, the Lynnhaven River, and Ewell Road.
- Section 2 (August 1956, Map Book 42, page 44) included both sides of Thoroughgood Drive and Hermitage Road from Westerfield Road to Five Forks Road.
- Section 3 (October 1956, Map Book 42, page 45) included the home sites between Thoroughgood Drive and Hermitage Road from Westerfield Road to Brooks Lane (i.e., Collier Lane).
- Section 4 (October 1956, Map Book 42, page 53) included the outer perimeter of Hermitage Road to Newgate Court, Reynolds Drive (both sides of the road), Adam Road, and Westerfield Road, to Five Forks Road.
- Section 5 (November 1956, Map Book 42, page 54) covered the outside of Thoroughgood Drive from Woodhouse (i.e., Maycraft) Road to Five Forks Road. The area included Curtiss Drive, Curtiss Court, and Burroughs Court.

THE BEGINNING

- Section 6 (November 1957, Map Book 44, page 38) covers the area in front of what would soon be the site for Thoroughgood Elementary School, to include Dunstan Lane and Austin Lane, bounded by Westerfield and Adam Roads.

Marketing the Thoroughgood Neighborhood. Sales brochures were impressive – color, oversized, and filled with actual photographs and artist's renderings of the area. Thoroughgood was advertised as "exclusive estate-size home sites situated in the heart of the historic Adam Thoroughgood Plantation." Goodman-Segar-Hogan was the sales agent for the property. The sales office was located at the entrance of Thoroughgood off Pleasure House Road at the end of Thoroughgood Square. The original sales office stands today and is presently occupied by the Virginia Independent Automobile Dealer's Association (VIADA). Six hundred twenty three homes were advertised on the original composite plat. Lot 1 was on the corner of Ewell and Stanfield on the east side of Stanfield just before the entrance to Ewell Point. Lot 623 was at the end of Five Forks Road, facing Curtiss Drive, backing up to Bayville Farm (i.e., Church Point). *(Note: Thorogood Corporation planned development of the 623 homes (sections 1-5) while James Collier was alive. Thorogood Corporation developed an additional 20 homes after James Collier's death. The 20 homes were developed as section 6 in December 1957. Clyde Collier – James' brother on behalf of Thorogood Corporation signed the section 6 plat.)*

Thoroughgood home sites were offered for sale *"for the discriminating"* homebuyer and its home sites "made possible country living in an area of Princess Anne County unsurpassed in beauty and rich in historical heritage." The brochure said "here homes will fit into the forest, here nature will be preserved and enhanced." Many of the native holly, dogwood, elm and oak trees were preserved during development. Features included waterfront home sites with superb views, wooded home sites in virgin forest, a private fresh water lake, boating facilities, excellent fishing, and convenient to Bay beaches. Although no longer available for all the residents, one long time resident recalled there was a boat ramp built. It was located near the corner of Country Club Circle and Arrowhead Point on what was referred to on the original plat on "Parcel B" – home site 249. It can be found today as the property on Arrowhead Point with a steep drop off to the inlet, where boat owners used to offload boats into Thoroughgood Cove. There was also

HISTORY OF THE THOROUGHGOOD NEIGHBORHOOD

mention of proposed riding facilities, and land reserved for a country club, neither of which reached fruition, possibly due to the death of James Collier. A junior high school was originally proposed on the original plat at the site currently occupied by Thoroughgood Elementary School. The advertisement promised property restrictions to protect the buyer's investment, and offered "genuine country living with city conveniences." To avoid undue concern to "Tidewater" (i.e., name precursor to "Hampton Roads") residents, the brochure assured its readers that "the Thoroughgood House would be restored both physically and in spirit." It promised, "the heartland acres of the Adam Thoroughgood Plantation would be dedicated to a community of quiet and beauty" and that the "beauty of the forest would be preserved and the homes would merge into the landscape." All and all Thoroughgood would be a "community in good taste, and a community which will be among the foremost in Virginia."

Marketing was also through the newspaper. One ad in 1958 (Ledger Dispatch-Star, Saturday Real Estate section) showed a picture of the wooded and gated front entrance with the headline "Thoroughgood – The Entrance to Your Future." Terms were $2,950 and up, with waterfront and wooded estate sized home sites. The ad boasted many values in modern, well-designed homes in Tidewater's most beautiful property; had access to boating-fishing-swimming, and was a highly respected suburban community."

The newspaper also ran full-length articles to profile different "Homes of the Week" in a variety of communities in the area – sometimes they were Thoroughgood homes. On Saturday, September 13, 1958, the Ledger Dispatch-Star profiled the home at 2820 Thoroughgood Drive. *Note: house numbering was different in those days – it is believed that 2820 might be 4104 Thoroughgood Drive today, based on the picture of the house in the ad.* The article described this home as situated in the middle of Thoroughgood's pecan grove, and said the home had all the "modern contributions to comfortable living." The home was a long rambling Colonial surrounded by 16 towering pecan trees on approximately one acre of land. The house had 2,600 feet of living space. The interior had an intercom installed in every area of the house – the must-have feature in those days. The state of the art intercom allowed two-way communication, plus piped in music. The kitchen was described as a "perfect command post" arrangement in which the lady of the house could prepare dinner, yet still remain an integral part of the family unit.

THE BEGINNING

Interior decorating reflected the tastes of that time - wallpaper was installed in the kitchen, dining room, and bathrooms. The family room had genuine western cedar paneling. Vinyl floors were used throughout for "easy housekeeping." As usual for Thoroughgood homes, a double oven was provided. The house offered plenty of baseboard radiation for an abundance of heat. The entry hall included a double closet with sliding doors for the "convenient handing of guests' apparel." The formal dining room had scenic wallpaper, chair rail, wainscot, and a crystal chandelier. The bathrooms were finished with mint green and cocoa ceramic tile, with a glass enclosure for the tub. The house had three "huge" bedrooms, two of which had double closets. The large solarium had 17 jalousie windows and a jalousie door. There were two fireplaces in the home. One hundred fifty ampere electric service was provided so that air conditioning could be installed "if desired." Lee A. Carlisle was the architect and builder and ran an ad accompanying the "Home of the Week" profile. He announced an open house that day for the home. The home was offered for $41,000 – and the builder would consider a "trade."

Property/Neighborhood Restrictions. Thorogood Corporation enforced the initial Declaration of Restrictions for the part of the neighborhood it developed. There were restrictions for erecting buildings (with proper distance from property lines) on the property without written approval from Thorogood Corporation. Fences also required the prior permission of the Thorogood Corporation, and according to long time residents, were difficult to get approved. As a result fences were almost non-existent in Thoroughgood at the time. The idea was to provide spacious properties in a natural woodland setting, and fences (however practical) did not fit into that description.

There were restrictions to forbid the raising of animals, livestock, or poultry, pertinent one supposes given the land used to be used for farming, and farming was still prevalent in Princess Anne County at the time. Restrictions forbade the use of asbestos or composition siding, or cement block of any kind. No trade or business could be carried on upon any site, other than the professional business of a doctor, dentist, architect, civil engineer, or lawyer, and forbade anything else that could become a nuisance or annoyance to the other residents. It did allow a guesthouse or cottage to be erected, with written approval from Thorogood Corporation. It was interesting to note that _suitable living quarters for domestic servants_ could be provided in any portion of a garage building erected on the property.

HISTORY OF THE THOROUGHGOOD NEIGHBORHOOD

There were separate deed restrictions for each section of Thoroughgood. Each version was similar, except that each excluded different properties in the section from the restrictions. For example, Section 1 deed restrictions exempted property around the Adam Thoroughgood House.

For some time, the Civic League pursued obtaining control of the restrictions from the Thorogood Corporation and the Colliers. In 1966 there was correspondence in the Civic League president's notes of a discussion between Hazel Fulford (formerly Hazel Collier) for the Civic League to take over deed restrictions. The Civic League agreed but Thorogood Corporation did not give authority at that time. It is unclear when the Colliers turned over the Deed Restrictions to the Civic League – it appeared to be sometime before 1982. This was not an easy or quick decision. As noted in League correspondence, the Collier sons said they held onto deed restrictions because they always wanted the place to look good – since their mom lived in the neighborhood and their dad developed it. To keep it looking good, however, in three or four instances the Colliers went to court with residents over fences or garages, and that was (likely) an unwanted burden. And it must have been cumbersome managing all those different versions of restrictions. The Civic League wanted the responsibility – they too had a vested interest to maintain property values, and perhaps they wanted one consolidated set of restrictions to apply equally to all homeowners. Plus at the time, they had a large, robust Board. For example, the Protection of Property Investment Committee of the Civic League in 1961 had a chairman and five committee members, and that was typical. However, the Civic League would also find out (after they finally assumed responsibility for deed restrictions) that enforcing them was no simple task. It was time-consuming, could be at times uncomfortably confrontational, and as a regulatory document, held insufficient legal recourse when residents refused to comply. Still, monitoring and enforcing restrictions remained a primary goal of the Civic League because it maintained the timeless elegance and consistently high property values of the neighborhood.

The Origin of Street Names. Street names are typically chosen by the property developer. The city registers the street name, checking for correct spelling and duplicates, but otherwise does not generally know anything about their origin. According to hearsay, the streets in Thoroughgood were named after the 105 indentured servants Adam Thoroughgood brought to this area. (Note: In Virginia there used to be what was called the "head rights"

THE BEGINNING

policy which gave 50 acres to each person paying his own way to settle in Virginia, plus 50 more for each "head," relative, or servant he brought along. Thus Adam Thoroughgood brought himself, his wife, and 105 indentured servants, and received 5,350 acres in return. This was one of the largest grants in Virginia colonial history. This policy and history was explained in an article in the Virginian Pilot written by Professor Dan Roberts, University of Richmond (date unknown, entitled "Head Rights Shaped Virginia") which reported that one of the ways Virginia saved itself in the difficult years after the settlement of Jamestown was to give land away to entice people to establish civilization in the wilderness.)

A list of those 105 names was obtained through Bob Perrine's book "Old Donation History" and was found to coincide to the neighborhood street names in many cases, as follows, with the original abbreviations. Some of the spelling is different, but close enough to be related:

- Chandler Lane – Tho. Chandler
- Westerfield Road – Jane Westerfield. By the way, the Virginian Pilot/Beacon (April 13, 2003) did a story on the Adam Thoroughgood House featuring Starr Plimpton - museum educator and living historian; also former wife of Steve Matton, Thoroughgood Civic League president, and daughter-in-law to another Thoroughgood Civic League president George Matton. Starr scripted and portrayed the fictional "life story" of Jane Westerfield, in an effort to explain the concept of indentured servitude for an event for the Adam Thoroughgood House. She described Jane as married to a baker, Tom. Tom, their two children and her mother burned to death in a London fire. Westerfield was forced to survive for a time by cleaning fish. While working down by the docks, Jane was intrigued by the splendid opportunity sailors claimed the New World offered. With nothing to keep her in London, she signed an indenture offering her labor in exchange for her passage. By the way, the article said that Starr Plimpton once lived on Westerfield Road.
- Keeling Landing Road – Thomas Keeling *(note: as identified in "Princess Anne County and Virginia Beach, a pictorial history" by Stephen S. Mansfield, Thomas Keeling was one of Adam Thoroughgood's 105 indentured servants. Adam Keeling, who built the Adam Keeling House in Virginia Beach, was Thomas' son.)*

HISTORY OF THE THOROUGHGOOD NEIGHBORHOOD

- Reynolds Drive – Edward or Jon. Reynolds
- Allerson Lane – Ann Allerson
- Wakefield Drive/Circle/Court – Jon. Wakefield
- Swaine Court – Stephen Swaine
- Westwell Lane – Robert Westwell
- Stanfield Road – Symond Stanfield
- Eggleston Court – Arthur Eggleston
- Atmore Lane – Thomas Atmore
- Whitethorne Road – possibly a variation of the name Ann Whitthorne
- Curtiss Drive/Court – possibly a variation of the name Eliza Curtisse
- Fraford Court – Victo Fraford
- Barnards Cove Road – perhaps for Stephen Bernard, or John Bernards
- Marshall Lane – Thomas Marshall (although Marshall Lane was not developed by the Colliers, so that may be a coincidence)

For the other streets names, a guess was made based on resident's memories and, in some cases deductive reasoning.

- Thoroughgood Drive. So named for the patriarch of the neighborhood – Adam Thoroughgood.
- Hermitage Road. Named after the Hermitage House located on the corner of Hermitage Road and Moores Lane.
- Ewell Road. Assumed named by and after the Ewell family that lived there.
- Country Club Circle. Named in anticipation of the proposed site of the Country Club planned to be erected at the end of Country Club Circle nearest the Adam Thoroughgood House – referred to as "Parcel A" on the original plat.
- Pecan Grove Road. Probably named after the pecan trees that flourished in that area. Pecan trees can still be seen lining ether side of Thoroughgood Lane approaching the Adam Thoroughgood House. That lane is particularly beautiful when the trees are in full bloom, and they provide a majestic natural entrance to the Adam Thoroughgood property.
- Burroughs Road. May have been attributed to Charles F. Burroughs, Jr. who owned nearby Bayville Farms - the present site of the Church Point neighborhood. Or may have been in honor of the two men named Burroughs were on the Board of the Adam Thoroughgood

THE BEGINNING

House Foundation. Or (more likely) it was in honor of the two Burroughs that were indentured servants of Adam Thoroughgood - William and Ann Burroughs.
- Parish Road. May have been related to Lynnhaven Parish, once located on adjoining land in present day Church Point, or may have been named after Edward Parish – one of Adam Thoroughgood's 105 indentured servants.
- Arrowhead Point. This street name might be related to the abundance of Indian arrowheads found on or nearby the road.
- Moores Lane. This private road is likely named after the owner of Moore's Farm, Ferrell Moore who lived at nearby Hermitage House. This road is physically linked to Swan Lake Road/Country Club Circle by an earth dam built to maintain Lake Charles at desirable levels.
- White Acre Road/Court. Likely named for the property that once stood as the birthplace and childhood home of esteemed Judge Benjamin Dey White. According to "Bayside History Trail, A View from the Water," the 167-acre farm in the vicinity of Independence Middle School was called "White Acres."
- Keeler Lane. Origin unknown, however, the owner of the Adam Thoroughgood House from 1906 – 1941 was Grace Keeler. Perhaps the lane pays homage to her. More about Miss Keeler in Chapter 8.
- Pleasure House Road. As provided in the Virginian Pilot's column "What's in a Name?" (July 20, 2007) Pleasure House Road refers to a tavern dating to the 1600s or 1700s, and not a brothel, as some may assume. The tavern was believed to be owned by the widow of Adam Thoroughgood, or to one of Thoroughgood's descendants. The tavern may have been located near the current road, perhaps at the old Bayville Farms, off First Court Road. Note: Pleasure House Road was also called Ocean Park Highway at one time.

Street Names that Changed. According to the original plat of the original rendering of the Thoroughgood neighborhood, some of the street names appear differently than we know them today. It is unclear when or why the name changed.

- Collier Lane was originally called "Brooks" Lane and extended across Hermitage Road. Brooks Lane might have been named after

HISTORY OF THE THOROUGHGOOD NEIGHBORHOOD

Thomas Brooks who was one of the 105 indentured servants Adam Thoroughgood brought to this area. Collier Lane was likely named after the developer of this neighborhood, James Collier, or the Collier family.

- Maycraft Road was originally called "Woodhouse" Road. In the 1959 Thoroughgood Civic League Directory, Gaston and Ozella Hudgins lived 1701 Woodhouse Road, and G. Smith lived at 1700 Woodhouse Road. Woodhouse Road is still referred to in the 1961 directory. The next available directory (1969) showed the use of "Maycraft" vs. "Woodhouse."

- Swan Lake Drive was originally called "Lake Charles" Road. Lake Charles Road is referred to in both the 1961 directory and again in 1974/75 Civic League files. This private road was renamed by Swan Lake Drive resident George Stenke in honor of the four pair of swans he brought to live on nearby Lake Charles.

- Adam Road was originally called "Wilsonn" (sic) Road. Wilsonn Road may have taken its name from James Wilson, one of the 105 indentured servants Adam Thoroughgood brought to this area. It is unclear if the name "Wilsonn Road" was ever used – the 1959 directory shows Jim and Millie Fisher living at 1802 Adam Road, Howard and Mary Stewart living at 1803 Adam Road, and Woodrow and Dorothy Martindale living at 1805 Adam Road.

- Stokes Court was originally called "Franklin" Court. Franklin Court may have been named after Henry Franklin, one of the 105 indentured servants Adam Thoroughgood brought to this area. Franklin Court was shown in the 1959 directory – a Commander and Mrs. Robert Bill was listed as living at 1601 Franklin Court, and John and Mary Ellis Compton lived at 1609 Franklin Court. Franklin Court is also listed in the 1961 directory. The next available directory (1969) showed the use of "Stokes" vs. "Franklin."

Five Forks Road. Looking at a 1945 Road Map of Princess Anne County available on the City of Virginia Beach's website, it appears that Five Forks Road pre-dated the Thoroughgood neighborhood. Five Forks Road on this map cuts across many large properties – they are abbreviated as "J. Dale," "W. Keeler," and "R TR TT" and appear to cover the original boundaries of Thoroughgood prior to the Ferrell Farm and Greenbrier Farms. Despite the

THE BEGINNING

abbreviations, it is thought that "J. Dale" refers to John Daley; "W. Keeler" refers to the Keeler family; and "R TR TT" refers to Dr. E. F. Truitt. The Truitt Farm was what is now known as Church Point. It was interesting to note that on this 1945 map, Five Forks Road extends to the Chesapeake Bay.

Note: it is wondered if this map is actually from an earlier time period than 1945. According to the personnel at the Adam Thoroughgood House, the Keeler family purchased their property in 1906. In 1941 Grace Keeler sold it to Thorowgood (sic) Manor, Inc. (Deed Book 209, page 33). Also, according to deed research done on the Hermitage House by Marianne Littel, John Daley sold his property to J. Wiley Halstead and John R. Simpson in 1923 (Deed Book 116, p. 349). Based on this information, the map could be anywhere from circa 1906 to 1923. When questioned about map dating for a different map offered on the same city website, city officials said the date could be confusing, and not related to all things on the map. For instance, the purpose of this 1945 map was to show roads in the area, and the map says it was revised in 1951. It could have super-imposed 1951 roads on earlier dated farmland. Regardless of the date – it shows interesting history of our area.

Today's Five Forks Road splits Thoroughgood in half, and it continues through the neighboring community of Lake Smith Terrace to the south. Also, as you will read in a future chapter, there was a "paper street" named Five Forks Road that continued north from its current end in Thoroughgood through Bayville Farms (i.e., Church Point).

It is not known where the name "Five Forks" comes from. The December 2012 edition of the *Lake Smith Ripples* (the newsletter for the Haygood Point/Lake Smith Terrace/Governor Square Civic League) says the name is related to the Battle of Five Forks, which was a Civil War battle fought near Five Forks in Dinwiddie County, Virginia on April 1, 1865. Five Forks referred to the intersection of four different roads, which formed five forks in the road. The battle was a loss for the Confederacy and began Robert E. Lee's retreat and eventual surrender at the Appomattox Court House on April 9, 1865. Five Forks is also the namesake of several towns and communities throughout Virginia.

<u>Private Roads</u>. Those yellow street signs in our neighborhood indicate a private road. The largest road that *used* to be private in Thoroughgood was Hermitage Point – more about that in Chapter 2. There are several private

HISTORY OF THE THOROUGHGOOD NEIGHBORHOOD

roads remaining in Thoroughgood – Moores Lane, Swan Lake Drive, Barnards Cove Road, Keeling Landing Road, Mallard Lane, and Allerson Lane. The City of Virginia Beach said although the streets are privately owned, they should be open to the general public unless the road is posted and/or gated with security pass. The city is generally not responsible for maintaining these private roadways.

Why private streets in a fully developed area? We don't know exactly. Virginia Beach city officials said some private roads have existed for many years and were platted as such when a property owner or owners wished to create a right of way or access for one or more property owners. The intent was to have those who own or used the road to provide the maintenance. Many private roads were established before there were governments to take care of minor roads.

Today, according to the Planning Department/Development Services Center Coordinator of the City of Virginia Beach, the private street question can be a complex one because of the lack of roadway construction standards in what was then Princess Anne County as opposed to the requirements of the modern roadway construction standards that now exist. There are sometimes legal issues regarding the ownership of the road and whether the developer can vacate the private road. Sometimes the roads are bypassed due to the legal issues associated with the ownership of the underlying fee. In some cases, the roads were improved and used for development. Today, developers wishing to create subdivisions using existing private roads or new private roads must seek a subdivision variance from City Council to allow lots to be created without direct access to an improved public street. If Council approves the request, the residents of the development will be responsible for the maintenance of the roads. Private roads are normal in condominium projects and apartments complexes. The residents usually expect to maintain the roads, parking, and drive aisle.

Sometimes residents in neighborhoods being served by a private street request the city take over maintenance and ownership of the street - such as what happened in Hermitage Point. The city says underlying ownership can be a legal stumbling block. If that is not a problem, the design of the road is often the insurmountable roadblock. It is the practice of the Departments of Public Works and Public Utilities to require the private street to be brought into compliance with all appropriate city ordinances and standard

THE BEGINNING

requirements before taking over ownership and maintenance of the street. In most cases, the upgrade of the street is cost prohibitive for the residents in the developments, which has been the case for some of the private roads in Thoroughgood. Even if residents would like to turn over the road to the city, it could be costly to first bring it up to city standards.

Telephone Numbers. The telephone number for Thoroughgood was initially HO4-XXXX. The "HO" letters represented a procedure used by the phone company back then to represent abbreviations for different telephone exchanges. Examples included the Madison exchange where numbers started with "MA" as in MA7-3655, or the Justice exchange where numbers started with "JU" as in JU7-8954, or the Ulysses exchange where numbers started with "UL" as in UL4-3758. If you look at a Princess Anne County phone directory, most all used the exchange format.

Speaking of the Justice exchange, when the Thorogood Corporation had their office in Norfolk on Military Highway, their number was JU8-3551. Goodman-Segar-Hogan Residential Sales Corporation (Thoroughgood's exclusive sales agent) was located on Granby Street in Norfolk and their number was MA5-4251, which was the Madison exchange.

The movie, *BUtterfield 8* starring Elizabeth Taylor was probably the most famous example of the existence of phone exchanges. The exchange abbreviation corresponded to numbers on the dial pad, so BUtterfield 8 (BU8) would have represented the prefix "288."

The "HO" number for Thoroughgood represented the "Howard" exchange. This was identified by a long time resident Anna Gray who used to work for C&P Telephone Company outside of the main entrance to Thoroughgood. The use of area codes eventually obviated the need to use exchanges, so the "HO4" prefix for Thoroughgood eventually became the more widely known "464" prefix. It is not sure when this happened because Thoroughgood Civic League Directories were not available each year – but in the 1969 directory, the numbers had shifted to the "464" prefix, vice the "HO4" prefix used in the 1961 directory.

Postal Address. It was confusing to note that the earliest sales agreement on file in League records for properties in Thoroughgood, referred to the lot or parcel of land as within the *Kempsville* District of Princess Anne County, Virginia. One might have thought that was a typographical error. However, in "An Economic and Social Survey of Various Virginia Counties" available

HISTORY OF THE THOROUGHGOOD NEIGHBORHOOD

at the University of Virginia, early Princess Anne County was made up of three districts – Seaboard, Kempsville and Pungo. Seaboard embraced the Town of Virginia Beach (i.e., area of the oceanfront), and was later divided into Seaboard and Lynnhaven. According to Dr. Stephen Mansfield, professor at Virginia Wesleyan College and a local expert on Princess Anne County, in 1958 the Kempsville Magisterial District broke up into Kempsville and Bayside. Long time Thoroughgood residents recall a postal address for Thoroughgood of "Bayside, Virginia" at one time. And, one resident also recalled a postal address of "Lynnhaven, Virginia" before that, but that was likely previous to the development of Thoroughgood.

In an article in the Virginian Pilot/Beacon (October 16, 1988), "Va. Beach's postal history is far from letter perfect" it was noted that in 1938 Virginia Beach did not have an official post office building. Back then all the postal windows operated from general stores and other commercial outlets – and once even out of an amusement park. The area did not really test the postal service until World War II when there was an influx of military, and then again after the 1963 merger of Virginia Beach and Princess Anne County. The article said most of the stations we are familiar with today began popping up after the war, beginning with the Bayside Station. Longtime Thoroughgood resident, Anne Greenberg, said her address on Ewell Road (prior to the development of the Thoroughgood neighborhood) was World's End Farm, vice a street address.

Old Fireplace at Entrance to Thoroughgood? During interviews for this book, there was talk of an old fireplace at the entrance to Thoroughgood. There were clues as to its existence while combing through Civic League records. In December 1974, for example, the Thoroughgood Civic League hosted a Christmas Carol Songfest and Bon-fire. Residents were told to bring the kids and gather around the "old fireplace" near the Thoroughgood entrance off Pleasure House Road. Shortly thereafter, the Thoroughgood Civic League President, Hank Pezzella sent a note of thanks to Mr. and Mrs. Danny L. Collier in appreciation for the use of their land and outdoor fireplace. In speaking to a long time resident, it was mentioned that the old fireplace was the remnant of a fire long ago that burned down a school that was located there. Sure enough, leafing through the book "A Collection of Newspaper Articles on the History of Princess Anne County, Virginia Beach, and Norfolk," there is a picture of the Skinner School, a school for black

THE BEGINNING

children. It was a medium sized structure, with white clapboard shingles, many windows, and a pitched roof. The picture shows students lined up with their teacher for some sort of outdoor activity. According to the William Skinner School Reunion booklet, dated July 1984, William Skinner was a Beachwood resident and member of nearby Morning Star Baptist Church. Sometime prior to 1923, he asked the Princess Anne County School Board to provide an adequate building to use as a school for the area's black children. Miss Grace Keeler was the owner of much land in Thoroughgood at that time, and she donated land at the current main entrance to Thoroughgood to Princess Anne County for the school. The school opened in 1923 to serve the children from Beachwood, Gracetown, Reedtown, Lake Smith, and Burton Station. The school closed in 1953. Local historian Edna Hendrix in her book "Black History: Our Heritage in Princess Anne County, Virginia Beach, Virginia," wrote that after the school closed, the school was meant to be moved to Gracetown for use as a recreational center, but it burned down (in 1954) before that could happen. The Reunion booklet said that in 1955, the Princess Anne County School Board sold the approximately 2 acres of land for $2,400. That sale was to James Collier (Deed Book 411, page 544) for the Thoroughgood neighborhood.

Thoroughgood Public Schools. Thoroughgood Elementary School (TES) opened in the fall of 1958. According to Sarah Aho (Historian for Virginia Beach Public Schools) the land transfer for TES was recorded in a Deed of Bargain and Sale from Thorogood Corporation for $3,600 dated January 1, 1958 (Deed Book 530, page 69). The architect was A. Ray Pentecost and the building cost $492,646 to build. The Virginia Beach Sun-News reported (September 4, 1958) that the inaugural opening for Thoroughgood Elementary School was delayed a few days as necessitated by Hurricane Daisy's "interference" with the construction of roads and walks at the school. The spokesman for the new school was none other than Frank W. Cox - then the Princess Anne County School superintendent. A picture of the newly opened school was provided in the Virginia Beach Sun-News (December 11, 1958). The caption called it an educational "plant" and said the general contractor was the Fred A. Haycox Company.

According to TES's website, during its first year, it housed eighth graders living in the northern section of (then) Princess Anne County. The students traveled to school via boat and bus, from points extending east to Oceana

◀ HISTORY OF THE THOROUGHGOOD NEIGHBORHOOD

and the Atlantic Ocean; and (curiously) the website said the students came from as far west as Ocean View, Larrymore Lawns, and Roosevelt Farms - those sections not then having been annexed by the City of Norfolk. The Sun-News article mentioned above said that the county would operate all schools in the Norfolk annexation area through the current school year that would end next June (1959). The following September the city of Norfolk would operate the schools in the newly annexed 13.5 square mile area for the first time. From 1959 – 1980, TES housed children in grades kindergarten through seven. In 1980, grade seven became part of the junior high school system.

Thoroughgood Elementary School has always been known for having a very strong and active PTA. The school's library houses scrapbooks made by the PTA to document the school's many functions and activities over each school year, with books found dating back to 1967. The pictures for that scrapbook included shots of students taken outside in what looked like to be a much broader campus – or at least one with less housing surrounding the school. The earliest known PTA for Thoroughgood was in 1960-61 – with Mr. Jesse Lunin as President. Before she was Thoroughgood Civic League President in 1988-89, Terri Dennis was also the President of Thoroughgood Elementary School's PTA in 1984-85.

As far as high schools are concerned, the Thoroughgood neighborhood was originally zoned for Princess Anne High School (PAHS). PAHS graduated its first class in 1954. A picture of the school at that time is available in the book "Virginia Beach in Vintage Postcards," by Alpheus J. Chewning, 2004. Looking at the school's aerial photograph, there is nothing but open land surrounding the school. The only sign of the city is the much smaller Virginia Beach Boulevard shown in front of the school. The area now occupied by Pembroke Mall was farmland.

Thoroughgood Civic League (TCL). In general, the neighborhood Civic League is a 20th century organization. Early Virginia Beach Civic Leagues were Glenrock and Oceana in the 1920s. The Thoroughgood Civic League was formed in 1957. The inkling of the beginning of the organization was mentioned in the Virginia Beach Sun-News (March 14, 1957). The article entitled "Thoroughgood News" reported "L. C. Burlage served as master of ceremonies at a 'get acquainted' cocktail hour held by Commander and Mrs. J. A. Wallace III, Saturday, March 2 at the Fort Story Officers Club."

THE BEGINNING

The article went on to list the approximately 44 Thoroughgood residents who attended the affair. These residents were the "plank-owners" of early Thoroughgood and included the Abernathy's, the Carharts, the Culpeppers, the Chandlers, the Langleys, the Hastings, and the Striblings. You will see these names referenced throughout this history.

As identified in the Constitution and By-laws, the purpose of TCL was "to bring into organization the residents and property owners of Thoroughgood to promote good fellowship, encourage interchange of ideas and further the best interest of this subdivision...toward beautification, recreation, sanitation, and safety of the residents, and protection of their property investments. The first president was L. Charles Burlage who served two terms – from 1957 to 1959. The fiscal year ran from June 1st to May 31st.

The elected officers and the executive Board, subject to the approval of the general membership, govern the Civic League. Early League records show active participation from a large and robust Board. For example the 1959 Board reflected 32 members comprising its officers and committees. The Membership and Attendance Committee had a chairman and eight committee members. The Protection of Property Investment Committee had a chairman and four committee members. There were also an Education and Program Committee and a Safety and Welfare Committee, staffed similar to the other committees. Committees varied over the years to meet the needs of the League – for example in 1968/69 there was a Directory Committee comprised of a chairman and eleven committee members. A Parliamentarian was always on hand to keep meetings in accordance with Robert's Rules of Order. Of special note were the duties of the Recording Secretary who kept the minutes of the meetings. These minutes were especially appreciated for the writing of this historical account of the neighborhood. They were immensely helpful in documenting the behind the scenes efforts of the Board in grappling with the many issues the neighborhood faced over the years. Without those notes, and the meticulous keeping of newspaper clippings and official correspondence of the time, this historical recap would not have been possible.

Appendix B provides a list of the former Civic League presidents, with additional information about them.

Thoroughgood Garden Club (TGC). Thoroughgood Garden Club was founded in 1957 by Mrs. A. H. (Olive) Culpepper, according to the club's

HISTORY OF THE THOROUGHGOOD NEIGHBORHOOD

historian, Joyce Barry. Mrs. Culpepper lived on Wakefield Drive and was the club's first President. The Virginia Beach Sun-News reported (March 14, 1957) that plans were made for the Garden Club on March 6, 1957 at the home of Mrs. S. W. Hastings on Hermitage Point, where Mrs. A. H. Culpepper presided at the meeting. At the time Mrs. Joseph McDonald was appointed chairman of the nominating committee. Serving with her was Mrs. J. A. Mullen, Jr., Mrs. Charles Martinette, Mrs. T. F. Jordan, and Mrs. L. C. Burlage. The next meeting was planned for April 10, 1957 at 8 p.m. at the home of Mrs. Gordon Smith on the corner of Wakefield Drive and Whitethorne Road.

TGC was featured in an article in the Virginian Pilot/Beacon (May 18, 1967) where it was said the club, then headed by Mrs. Taylor (Anna) Gray of Swaine Court, installed two lights and a scroll of ironwork with the name "Thoroughgood" atop the brick pillars that mark the entrance off Pleasure House Road. At the time of the article two more lights had been ordered, bringing the total to four carriage lights along with an electronic light meter. The article also said the garden club worked to beautify the post office at Bayside. In a Virginian Pilot article (May 22, 1969), the TGC was noted for clearing and beautifying the picnic area at the Hermitage School. During this timeframe, the garden club held an April garden tour of the outstanding gardens of Thoroughgood.

Thoroughgood Garden Club is a federated garden club and is a member of the National Council of State Garden Clubs, the Virginia Federation of Garden Clubs (VFGC), and the Tidewater District of the VFGC and the Council of Garden Clubs of Virginia Beach. The Bylaws of the Thoroughgood Garden Club state: "The object of this club shall be to promote the love of gardening among amateurs, to protect our native birds, to encourage Civic planting and beauty, to share with others - plants, bulbs and roots - and to cooperate in projects for conservation, beautification, cleanliness and sanitation."

TGC has been a great supporter of the Thoroughgood Civic League with many financial donations in support of the neighborhood for the last 56 years. The two organizations have worked hand in hand together on various projects, including the main entrance and the brick entrances at Five Forks Road and Ewell Road; the gardening at the three entrances; landscaping at the various pumping stations in the neighborhood; and gardening at

THE BEGINNING

the brick sidewalls at either side of the front entrance. The club installed the crepe myrtle trees in the center of the main entrance; ornamental pear trees on Independence Boulevard (gone now); trees at the southern tunnel entrance; wildflowers on Northampton Blvd; plantings at Thoroughgood School; and provided donations and holiday decorating for the Adam Thoroughgood House. The club provided donations to the Council of Garden Clubs of Virginia Beach, Norfolk Botanical Gardens, Rescue Squads, and two neighborhood schools. In 1966/67, as mentioned above TGC coordinated the installation of two post lights on the brick pillars flanking the entrance to Thoroughgood and installed the scroll of ironwork with the name "Thoroughgood" on the center structure between the brick pillars.

TGC has consistently held fund-raisers for charity, community organizations, and local beautification projects since its inception. For approximately 15 years a Holiday House was held the first weekend in December at a member's home with a tour of the decorated home, a gift/craft bazaar, and a bake sale. On occasion there was a cookbook available. Presently the TGC holds fund-raisers in the spring offering plants, garden decor, cookbooks, crafts and baked goods. The Holiday sale during the first weekend of December includes freshly made holiday greenery, wreaths, table decor, crafts, and baked goods. These events are typically held on the grounds of the Adam Thoroughgood House.

Among awards the club has won from the Council of Garden Clubs is the Home and Neighborhood Development Service (HANDS) awards. The club enjoys programs at the meetings from various speakers as from the Marine Science Museum, the City of Virginia Beach Water Conservation, Bird Conservation and Backyard Wildlife Habitat, Chrysler Museum, Tidewater Iris Society and various Florist Shops.

Hermitage Garden Club. According to Mrs. Barry who is also a member of this club, the Hermitage Garden Club of Virginia Beach was formed April 22, 1966 and the first President was Mrs. B. M. (Nell) Cuthrell, Jr. who lived on Hermitage Road. The meetings are held once a month at Bayside Presbyterian Church. Their object: "To share and promote interest in horticulture and use of flowers in the home." The club is not federated. During the 1960s, some members of the Thoroughgood Garden Club preferred a daytime club and so the Hermitage Garden Club was formed. Civic League notes show that in the past HGC contributed funds to the Civic League for

◄ HISTORY OF THE THOROUGHGOOD NEIGHBORHOOD

the maintenance and care of the front entrance. Also in 1997, the HGC provided wreaths to decorate Thoroughgood Square.

Local Commerce Outside the Neighborhood at the Time of Development.

- The area from Pleasure House Road to Bayside Shopping Center (at intersection of Pleasure House Road and Shore Drive). We were not able to find exactly what existed in this section of town in the 1950s. However, according to an aerial photograph of the area in 1966, the churches and businesses included Morning Star Baptist Church (founded in 1892), Bayside Baptist Church, Bayside Pharmacy, and three eating establishments (Shore Drive Inn, Min's, and Burger Chef). Bayside Pharmacy closed in 2002 and was featured in an article in the Virginian Pilot/Beacon (September 29, 2002). The Bayside Shopping area featured S&S Five-and-Dime Store, hardware store, Colonial (Food) Store, filling station, two cleaning establishments, two used car auto sales (one was McCoy Motors Company), two auto repair establishments (one was Few's Body and Collision Shop), Virginia National Bank, a loan company, Post Office Branch 23455 (then located where Weathersby's is today), two medical buildings, beauty shop, barber shop, bakery, TV sales and service shop, auto parts shop, and Bayside Bowling Alley (later a skating rink and where Grand Affairs is today).
- Near Bayside Shopping Center was the Shore Drive Inn. According to picture and caption in "A Collection of Newspaper Articles on the History of Princess Anne County, Virginia Beach and Norfolk," W. W. Oliver built the Shore Drive Inn at the corner of Shore Drive and Pleasure House Road in the 1930s. There is evidence in League records that some membership meetings were held there prior to 1963. A letter dated March 16, 1963 from then Thoroughgood Civic League president Elwood Braunbeck to Mrs. Hogge at the Shore Drive Inn, thanked her for her kind hospitality, but due to an increase in membership (up to 165) the Thoroughgood Civic League would be unable to use their facilities that year.
- Casino Restaurant was highlighted in an article in the Beacon (June 10, 1981). It was regarded as a Chesapeake Beach landmark for forty years, and known for its burgers. The article was warning of its

THE BEGINNING

possible demise related to potential rezoning in the area that would allow the construction of townhouses on the site.

- Shore Drive-In Theater was located just off Northampton Boulevard on Shore Drive. In an article in the Virginian Pilot (September 3, 1961), the theater manager said it opened in 1956, and could accommodate 800 automobiles. In 1961 a large pepperoni pizza was $1.45 and ice cream was $.10. It was open year round, but understandably saw its largest crowds in the summer. In those days the drive-in theaters were 80 percent family trade, which is why the Shore Drive-In had pony rides, playground equipment..... and bottle warmers!
- Two hotels used to exist on Page Avenue near the Lesner Bridge – The Sunset Motel and the Ocean Air Motel. Travelers who got off the ferry from the Eastern Shore and didn't want to travel all the way to the oceanfront often used them. Nearby was Duck-In Restaurant, which began in 1952, and closed in 2005. In addition there was the Seven Seas Seafood Restaurant, which opened in 1963 and closed in 1973.
- Two other restaurants – Hurd's on the Lynnhaven River – opened in 1936 and closed in 1984, and (Tandom's) Pine Tree Inn on Virginia Beach Boulevard. Tandom's was where one of the Civic League annual dinners was held. Tandom's opened in 1927 and stayed in business for nearly 70 years.
- The area of Pleasure House Road to Robbins Corner (at the intersection of Pleasure House Road and Independence Road, formerly Bayside Road). A longtime resident remembered Robbins Corner Grocery and Meat Market as the place for Princess Anne County officials to get together and make decisions about the County. As noted in "Bayside History Trail, A View from the Water" Church Point was the site of one of the first courthouses in Princess Anne County. There is no full recap of stores at Robbins Corner in the late 1950s, but a 1966 aerial photograph showed Robbins Corner to be quite large, spanning both sides of Bayside Road (i.e., Independence Boulevard) at Pleasure House Road. In 1966, the following commercial businesses existed between the Thoroughgood Entrance (on Pleasure House Road) and Robbins Corner: C&P

25

◄ HISTORY OF THE THOROUGHGOOD NEIGHBORHOOD

Telephone Company (now Verizon and still stands in original location), two doctors/dentist buildings, three filling stations, three markets (Robbins Corner Grocery, Farm Fresh and 7-11), two beauty shops, three cleaning establishments, two barber shops, two insurance offices, two eating establishments, two TV and/or electronics shops, hardware store, antique shop, second-hand store, fuel oil station, heating and plumbing shop, florist and gift shop, piano school, dance school, yard and fabric shop, Block's Income Tax Service, and First and Merchant's National Bank. Another long time resident recalled there was a small hot dog store on the corner of Independence and Pleasure House called BJ's Hot Dogs. All the young people would meet there from this neighborhood. According to a Virginian Pilot/Beacon article on the 25th Anniversary of Virginia Beach (February 24, 1988) BJ's Hot Dogs used to be called Allie's Stop-In during the 1950s.

Roadways Around Thoroughgood in the 1950s. The neighborhood marketing brochure for Thoroughgood showed an overview of major roads and points of interest. Not all the roads are searchable today – some may have been re-routed when I-64 or other large roads were built. The picture showed Route 58 (Virginia Beach Boulevard) stretch from downtown Norfolk to the Oceanfront – and it still does. Shown as an offshoot of Route 58 was Route 44, which eventually became I-264. It showed Route 60 (Shore Drive) hugging the coast (as it does now) from Willoughby to the Oceanfront. It showed Route 13Y starting in downtown Norfolk and ending at the Chesapeake Bay – research indicates this might have been both Water Works Road and Shell Road, but eventually would turn into Northampton Boulevard leading to the Chesapeake Bay Bridge Tunnel when it was later built. It showed Route 160 from the Norfolk Naval Base, which turned into Route 168 (Tidewater Drive) ending at its intersection with Route 13. It showed Route 165 (Military Highway) crossing Route 58 (Virginia Beach Boulevard) and ending at its intersection with Route 168. The map showed Norfolk International Airport as a "Municipal Airport."

- The neighborhood brochure map showed the distance to Princess Anne High School for which Thoroughgood was zoned initially. It is not certain what elementary school Thoroughgood was zoned for prior to Thoroughgood Elementary School being built in 1958.

THE BEGINNING

Longtime resident Andy Mullen says it was Shelton Park Grammar School. This makes sense, because the neighborhood map's only reference to an elementary school was in showing the distance to Shelton Park Grammar School.

- It is not clear when Northampton Boulevard was built, but it was built to lead to the Chesapeake Bay Bridge Tunnel, which opened in 1964. Previous to the tunnel, a ferry took passengers to the Eastern Shore. One ferry was called the "Gateway to the North" and the Virginia Beach side was located off Diamond Springs Road and Shore Drive at Route 13. It carried 80 cars, buses, and 45 trucks, as well as 1,000 people, and ran every two hours. A picture of the ferry and information about it is in the book "A Collection of Newspaper Articles on the History of Princess Anne County, Virginia Beach, and Norfolk." There was another ferry connecting Cape Charles to Little Creek (as depicted in the C. Michelle Norton postcard collection, Virginia Beach Public Library) operated by the Virginia Ferry Corporation, and was in operation from 1933 to at least the early 1950s. Their three transport ships were called the S. S. Pocahontas, S. S. Princess Anne, and S. S. DelMarVa. The ad said their modern fast steamers covered the trip in an hour and forty-five minutes, with a boat operating every 90 minutes. The ad then (curiously) noted that gasoline was not drained from cars for this trip. In 1956, the ferry service was taken over by the Chesapeake Bay Ferry Commission. One purpose of the commission was to study the feasibility of building a bridge to replace the ferries.

- By the way, in the Virginian Pilot neighborhood profile of Thoroughgood (May 18, 1967) noted that in 1636, Adam Thoroughgood was credited with establishing the first ferry in Lower Norfolk, a service that was America's oldest until it was replaced by a tunnel in 1952. In the book "Lost Virginia Beach," Amy Waters Yarsinski explains the ferry service was positioned at the convergence of the eastern and southern branches of the Elizabeth River between Norfolk and Portsmouth. Ms. Waters Yarsinski said the ferry was nothing fancy – it was a small skiff handled by his slaves. But it was so popular within a few months the county took over his enterprise, adding more rowboats.

- Bayside Road was later expanded into present day Independence Boulevard. City of Virginia Beach Public Works Engineer and long

HISTORY OF THE THOROUGHGOOD NEIGHBORHOOD

time Thoroughgood resident Jeff Waller said that Independence Boulevard by Pembroke Mall as it connected to Virginia Beach Boulevard was under construction in late 1965 and probably finished in 1966. He believed that prior to finishing, Independence Boulevard (then called Bayside Road) went south from Ewell Road to Witchduck Road. If you wanted to go to Virginia Beach Boulevard you had to go via Witchduck Road.

- Shore Drive (Route 60) existed. According to the book "Princess Anne County and Virginia Beach, a pictorial history" by Stephen S. Mansfield, Shore Drive opened in 1928 with the intention to relieve some of the congestion on Virginia Beach Boulevard. The problem was the Lesner Bridge was a drawbridge. On one Sunday afternoon in 1949, the drawbridge opened 87 different times to allow small boats to pass through the inlet. The present, draw-less Lesner Bridge was completed in 1958.
- According to the book "The Beach" Virginia Beach Boulevard existed – although fewer lanes than today. It was built in 1921, as the first concrete, hard-surfaced road from Norfolk to Virginia Beach. The creation of this roadway was a big event as discussed in an article in the Beacon (July 21, 1985). The article said when the road opened in 1921 it was heralded as Virginia's "Appian Way" – a name taken from the oldest and best preserved of the Roman roads. Highway officials said it was built to serve mankind equally as long as the Roman road. The opening of the road was celebrated with a "sociability run," sponsored by the Tidewater Automobile Association. A procession of more than 500 cars (and 1,500 people) took part in the "run," which began at 21st Street and Colonial Avenue in Norfolk, went down the new road and ended at the Casino on the oceanfront. All along the route, wherever there were houses, residents had decorated the buildings with flowers and bunting in honor of the event. Flags flew from every gatepost in the little town of Oceana. Princess Anne County farmers suspended work for the afternoon and brought their families to the roadside, waited for the procession to pass, and joined the stream of cars. It was humorous to note that there was a special division for cars driven by women. This division was provided with special precautions against accidents. At the end of the run, there were social

functions for the participants. The new Princess Anne Country Club was opened to the group, as was the new bathing pavilion at the Virginia Beach Casino.

Virginia Beach Council of Civic Organizations (VBCCO). According to their website, the VBCCO was founded in 1959 as a way to ensure that all citizens had a voice in local governance. In his obituary, L. Charles Burlage – Thoroughgood Civic League's first president – was listed as the co-founder of VBCCO. As of 2012, VBCCO represented over 100 Civic organizations (not just Civic Leagues, but included women's clubs, garden clubs, etc.) throughout Virginia Beach. VBCCO was chartered to educate member Civic Leagues about how to improve their community and how to ensure their voice is heard. The VBCCO unites the people of Virginia Beach communities, and studies their problems. They conduct regular educational programs, and provide a citywide forum for a full and free discussion of any Civic, governmental, commercial question. Thoroughgood Civic League was a long-time member of VBCCO, and usually sent a delegate to VBCCO meetings – who reported back Virginia Beach Civic events of interest to our community.

CHAPTER 2

Neighborhood Anchors

Arrowhead, Hermitage, and Ewell Points anchor the Thoroughgood neighborhood along its eastern boundary along the Lynnhaven River. There is much rich history in those (and nearby) surrounding areas.

Arrowhead Point. Arrowhead Point gets its name related to the discovery of Indian arrowheads on/close by this location. Arrowhead Point and nearby Country Club Circle was Collier territory.

James Collier was the president of Thorogood Corporation. A 1955 advertisement for the Thoroughgood House listed the office for Thorogood Corporation as 7413 Military Highway, but later correspondence showed 301 Lynnhaven Parkway in Virginia Beach. Just prior to purchase of the Thoroughgood property in 1955, a Virginian Pilot newspaper article (December 23, 1954) reported Mr. Collier as president of the Eastern Realty Development Corporation – which at that time was in the midst of erecting a new subdivision of about 50 homes in Bay Lake Pines on Lake Joyce.

Mr. Collier married Hazel Dixon. Mr. and Mrs. Collier had four children – Kay Francis Collier Davis was the oldest, followed by sons James (Jimmy) Dixon, Daniel (Danny) LaRay, and W. (William) Richard Collier.

Mr. Collier died on May 15, 1957, along with three others in a plane crash over Hatteras Inlet, North Carolina. The crash was reported in an article in the Virginian Pilot (May 17, 1957). It was a horrific family tragedy. The article reported four men were killed – James N. Collier, Russell L. Wommack, Arthur B. Harriman, and Henry D. Mozingo, Jr. The four men were close friends through marriage between their families, and with common social and business interests – Mr. Harriman was married to a sister

◄ HISTORY OF THE THOROUGHGOOD NEIGHBORHOOD

of Mr. Wommack; Mr. Collier was married to a sister of Mr. Mozingo; and Mr. Mozingo was married to a sister of Mr. Collier. All four had interests in the same real estate enterprises in the Norfolk area. The plane belonged to Consolidated Construction Company. Mr. Collier had been the pilot of the fateful flight, having had a pilot's license for about four years.

Mr. Collier was 38 at the time of his death, and left behind his 37-year-old wife and children whose ages ranged from 12 to 17, along with a large neighborhood in its infancy of development. At the time of his death his address was listed as 400 Bayville Road, in Baylake Pines. Mr. Collier was listed as a native of Smithfield, North Carolina.

After Mr. Collier's death, the Internal Revenue Service would not allow some of his plans (i.e., country club) to be completed. The corporation was allowed to remain open only until the remaining lots were sold. A Virginian Pilot article (September 23, 1957) reported that Clyde L. Collier, brother of James was named president of Thorogood Corporation with Mrs. J. N. Collier as vice president. In the article, Mr. Clyde Collier announced that no change in the corporation policies were contemplated, and said the boat dock for the convenience of Thoroughgood residents had been completed.

Sadly, this was not the only tragedy the Collier family had to face. As reported in the Virginian Pilot (September 3, 1961), the Collier's oldest son – James D. was killed in an automobile collision on Route 60 near the Fort Story gate on September 2, 1961. He was age 20 at the time.

At some point Mrs. Collier married F. William Fulford of Fulford Realty and Fulford Construction Company. Mr. Fulford was previously in the Navy and served in World War II and Korea. Mr. Fulford died at age 56 on October 18, 1981. Mrs. Collier/Fulford died at age 74 on November 25, 1993. Her obituary (reported in the Virginian Pilot, November 26, 1993) said she was a homemaker and mother and member of Our Savior's Lutheran Church, and had eight grandchildren at the time of her death. Daughter Kay Collier passed away on January 29, 2011 at the age of 71. Kay Collier's obituary said one of her interests was in the preservation of the Adam Thoroughgood House. Son James D. (Jimmy) Collier died tragically on September 2, 1961 as mentioned above. Son Danny Collier fell from a deer stand and sustained serious injuries. The Virginian Pilot obituary (August 15, 1998) reported he died at age 55 on August 14, 1998. The obituary said he was a hunter, fisherman, sportsman, and an avid wildlife conservationist. As of the time of this writing, the only living child of James and Hazel Collier is Richard Collier.

According to directories and correspondence over time, the Collier family lived in and around Arrowhead Point, as follows:

- Mrs. Collier lived at 1810 Arrowhead Point, listed as living at that address in the 1959 and 1961 Thoroughgood Civic League Directories.
- In the 1969 Thoroughgood Civic League Directory, William and Hazel Fulford are listed as living at 1617 Arrowhead Point. It is not clear if 1617 Arrowhead Point is a different house than 1810 Arrowhead Point, but in the 1969 directory, there are no houses numbered in the 1800s on Arrowhead Point – it appears the house numbers changed to the 1600 series for some reason - perhaps related to the change of address for the general area from Bayside, Virginia to Virginia Beach, Virginia. Also, oddly, in the 1970 directory, the couple is listed as living 4625 Curtiss Court. But then in the 1978 directory, the Fulford's address is back to 1617 Arrowhead Point and Civic League correspondence with Mrs. Fulford in 1984 shows her still at that address. It is not known whether the Fulfords ever lived on Curtiss Court, but they were deeded that property in 1969, and sold it in 1970.
- Kay Collier lived at 4344 Country Club Circle.
- Danny Collier, and his wife Johnnie Mae initially lived at 4729 Bradston Road as reported in the 1970 Thoroughgood Civic League Directory. A letter from the Civic League to Danny Collier in 1975 listed his and Johnnie Mae's address at 4109 Country Club Circle (part of the original Parcel B on Country Club Circle). In the 1978 directory, Danny and Johnnie Mae Collier are listed as living at 4332 Country Club Circle. And then in some League correspondence with Danny Collier and his wife in 1985, Danny's address was 4007 Arrowhead Point Court.
- W. Richard Collier and his wife Berry were the only part of the family not living in or near Arrowhead Point. They lived at 1505 Westerfield Road (as listed in the 1969 directory), and then at 4420 Delray Drive (as noted in a letter from Richard Collier to the Civic League in 1975). As of 1985, League correspondence showed that Richard and Berry Collier moved to Baylake Pines.

HISTORY OF THE THOROUGHGOOD NEIGHBORHOOD

Houses of note near Arrowhead Point:

- **_Adam Thoroughgood House_**. As was already mentioned in the previous chapter, James Collier conveyed the Adam Thoroughgood House and surrounding land to the Adam Thoroughgood Foundation in 1955. The house was managed by Chrysler Museum and the City of Norfolk until 2003 when it was turned over to the City of Virginia Beach. The house was originally thought to have been built around 1636 and billed as the oldest English brick home in America. Henry Clay Hofheimer (President of the Adam Thoroughgood House Foundation) saw to a thorough renovation of the house and gardens in 1957. Mr. Hofheimer spent quite a bit of time and money to scavenge the towns and cities of Europe for appropriate period furnishings. As a result, the small four-room house was beautifully equipped. The staff of the Adam Thoroughgood house dressed in period costumes and did a wonderful job recounting Colonial life experienced by the Thoroughgood's in their day. It has been a popular attraction for residents, school children, and tourists. The Beacon wrote an article on the neighborhood (May 17, 1967), and in it said that the elegant lawn and gardens of the Adam Thoroughgood House set the standard for most of the yards of residents in the community. The Beacon article recounted a humorous story. Martha Lindemann, curator and hostess of the Adam Thoroughgood House at that time also had her residence across the street at 1641 Parish Drive. There had been claims over time that the ghost of Sarah Thoroughgood walked in the evening with a lighted candle. However, Martha noted that she, in her 17th Century gown on occasion returned home in the twilight hours bearing a lighted candle. It was likely the "ghost" rumors were really just her going home after work.
- **_"Dream" House_**. As mentioned above, the Colliers lived at 1810 Arrowhead Point. This home is no longer standing and there is no "1810" address any longer but it stood on the second plat of land to the immediate right upon turning into Arrowhead Point Court. The address likely changed to 1617 Arrowhead Point after the merger of Princess Anne County with the Town of Virginia Beach in 1963. Their house was the model home for the neighborhood initially, and referred to as the "dream house." A longtime resident and real

estate professional said that it is common to name model homes. A Virginian Pilot article (September 23, 1957) reported that the widely publicized $150,000 "dream house" had been completed, and had attracted thousands of visitors. According to later real estate reports, the house was 4,000 square feet red brick ranch on four acres, and had a pool, bulkhead and pier.

- **Swan Lake Drive**. The owner of this private road, along with the Earth Dam that shores up Lake Charles is George Stenke. Mr. Stenke and his wife Josephine (since passed) came to live in Thoroughgood in May 1961, and built a beautiful home on two lots on Swan Lake Drive. Before building his house he widened the dam by 100 feet. When he moved here, he recalled that the interior of Country Club Circle was nothing but a cleared field with a barn at one end. Swan Lake Drive was called Lake Charles Road on the neighborhood plat, but Mr. Stenke always knew it as Moores Lane when he built here – perhaps a continuation of the Moores Lane to the south of the dam. Mr. Stenke changed the name to Swan Lake Drive in honor of the eight swans he purchased to make their home in Lake Charles years ago. Longtime residents recall driving over the dam in their cars, or having picnics or fishing from the dam prior to it becoming private. Mr. Stenke said the mail truck also used to cross the dam. Purchased in 1982, Mr. Stenke currently owns and maintains both the eastern and western sides of the earth dam, while Mr. Stenke says that Thorogood Corporation (*or the Collier Estate*) owns the fee in the dam. At the edge of the dam is a miniature lighthouse that flanks Thoroughgood Cove. *Note: At the top of the lighthouse is a light that was originally emergency warning light used in the Farm Fresh Supermarket bakery previously located on Azalea Garden Road in Norfolk.* Mr. Stenke said in 1963 Hurricane Hazel caused Lake Charles to overflow into Thoroughgood Cove. He called a meeting of all lakefront residents to discuss options. To correct the situation, he had the city build three spillways and he built a bulkhead on both sides of the dam. Mr. Stenke has a fountain on the water near his house that aerates the water near his house to reduce the algae that grows in the lake and keeps the fish alive. A year or two ago the Corps of Engineers was considering a plan to remove dams in the

HISTORY OF THE THOROUGHGOOD NEIGHBORHOOD

Lynnhaven River (including Lake Charles) and have upstream lakes revert to salt water and plant oyster beds. There was a public meeting in Great Neck area and there was much public outcry and this plan was dropped. Mr. Stenke also (at one time) owned the lot on the south side of the dam in back of the Hermitage House (lot 38 on the neighborhood plat). Read more on George Stenke in Chapter 8.

Hermitage Point. Hermitage Point and Hermitage Road are named in honor of the Hermitage House located at 4200 Hermitage Road. When Hermitage Point was first developed, the residents on the point owned the road – and the road was gravel poured over hot tar. This type of road was different than the non-private roads. The road started immediately after the dip in the road at the entrance to Hermitage Point. Looking at the original plat, there was not a road as one would normally see on a neighborhood plat, just housing plats that butted up against each other on the front, right, and left. The houses also did not have the typical postal address. For example, what is known today as 4133 Hermitage Point ("Shelter Quay") was originally known as 13 Hermitage Point. The origination of the numbering is a bit of a mystery since 13 Hermitage Point was not lot 13 but rather it was lot 15 on the neighborhood plat.

Although there are about 30 lots on Hermitage Point, until the late 1950s only five families lived there – the Abernathy's were the first to build (6 Hermitage Point), followed by the Hastings (18 Hermitage Point), Langleys (7 Hermitage Point), Carharts (11 Hermitage Point), and the Mullens (13 Hermitage Point). Andy Mullen was a young child when his family moved here in on January 2, 1957, and he still lives in, and fastidiously cares for the same house today. He was kind enough to share some of his memories of the area.

Because of the unique issues related to maintaining a large private road, the residents of Hermitage Point created their own "mini" Civic League. It was called the "Hermitage Point Neighbors" and held its first meeting in December 1956 at the Abernathy home. The minutes from that meeting showed a pleasant relationship with James Collier in answering Hermitage Point resident concerns about the road. Eventually, the residents turned the road over to the city to maintain as related to installing city water in the late

NEIGHBORHOOD ANCHORS

1960s. Otherwise, the city would not have run water pipes down a private road of that length.

Perhaps because of that initial bonding over road concerns, this small close-knit community developed traditions that continue to this day – including a Christmas cocktail party, door to door Christmas caroling by the school age children, and a Fourth of July picnic. Hermitage Point residents took turns hosting the events, but for a time the picnics were held at the Rawls' house who owned the two lots at the very end of Hermitage Point. One lot was for their house, but the other lot was left vacant and used to play baseball, basketball, and shuffleboard. Mr. Rawls was part owner in a building supply business (Seaboard Paint and Supply Company) and had his employees build eight to ten picnic tables to use for the picnics. Mrs. Rawls was an artist who painted landscapes – some of which were scenes from her property on Hermitage Point and Lynnhaven River.

Mr. Mullen remembers a much less populated Thoroughgood when he was a boy. He recalled an idyllic life, similar to the old TV show "Leave it to Beaver." His father bought he and his brother a $5 rowboat to spend summers on the river. The brothers and their friends crabbed, fished, and waterskied. They built tree forts on the vacant lots. In the winter, the neighborhood kids would sled on two Hermitage Point lots – one that had a steep decline into both the river and onto the adjoining property. The Powers owned one of the lots. Mr. Powers provided use of the oil drum with firewood to warm cold snow encrusted hands, while Mrs. Powers provided hot chocolate for the children. The Gallop neighbors provided winter fun too. Mr. Gallop would hook sleds to his car by rope and pulled the kids down Hermitage Point. Mrs. Gallop was a teacher at Thoroughgood Elementary School at the time. Mr. Mullen said the area south of Hermitage Road between Stanfield, Whitethorne, and Ewell was a big open field where corn and wheat was once grown. It was devoid of trees – a sharp contrast to the many mature trees across the street at the Hermitage House. There was a large white barn on the corner of Hermitage and Whitethorne used for the farming activities. Mr. Mullen recalled the tunnel of trees on Ewell Road, hoards of beautiful butterflies in the area, and peacocks at White Acre farm.

Mr. Mullen remembered one more thing too. The entrance to Hermitage Point currently has brick columns, but used to have a custom made stained wooden sign next to the right column with gold lettering to announce

HISTORY OF THE THOROUGHGOOD NEIGHBORHOOD

Hermitage Point. The sign included the names of all the residents – in the order in which their houses occurred on the Point. The residents had the sign made.

Other points of interest nearby Hermitage Point included:

Hermitage Road. According to an article in the Virginia Pilot/Beacon (November 14, 1998), Hermitage Road began as a farm lane with collards, kale and corn raised for seed on either side. The corn was dried in the barn, which was also home to mules Kate and Lily. Claire McDermott, Thoroughgood resident was interviewed for the article and said remnants of a barn foundation could still be found behind her Hermitage Road home. And, she said, signs of silos were behind her neighbor's house.

Hermitage House. We don't just have one historic home in our neighborhood – we have two. According to the *"50 Most Historically Significant Houses and Structures in Virginia Beach,"* the Hermitage House is circa 1699 with additions in 1834 and 1940. John Thoroughgood built the house on his portion of Adam Thoroughgood's Grand Patent. It originally consisted of two rooms downstairs, and one room upstairs. In 1805 a basement was dug, and bricked in – likely intended as a cistern to catch rainwater. In 1834 the Woodhouse family added federal style crown molding, recessed panel wainscoting throughout the house and a central passage. In 1940 indoor plumbing was added along with a new wing in which a kitchen, and maid's room was built downstairs, and a bedroom, and two baths built upstairs. The last owner of the house prior to the Collier's development of Thoroughgood was Ferrell Moore, who farmed on his surrounding 330 acres. Back then, the approach to the original farmhouse stretched from Pleasure House Road to Independence, and the 1.5 mile approach to the house used to be lined with lilacs. Outbuildings on the property predated the Civil War and included a pump/milk house, a smokehouse and a garage that was once the stable, kitchen or both. Current owner Marianne Littel has a full list of past owners of the Hermitage House – a few of the more recent ones include:

- Ferrell and Linda Moore purchased the house in 1940. The Virginian Pilot did a profile of the house (March 27, 1955), just prior to the sale of the house to Mr. Collier that same year. The article was written by none other than Louisa Venable Kyle, who was the official raconteur and historian of Princess Anne County. A picture accompanied the article, and the house was shown with a small covered front porch with two columns with wrought iron railings. A picture was provided of Mrs. Moore sitting by the living room fireplace. The road leading to the house was described as wooded, with herons and snowy egrets to be seen, and the long approach lined with lilac bushes. There were fertile fields kept under cultivation year round. Another Virginian Pilot article on the house (February 21, 1955) reported that Mr. Moore was the president of D. W. Warren Company, Inc. It was the Moore's who sold the home and 313.9 acres of surrounding land in Thoroughgood to Mr. Collier.

- The Ledger Star did an article on the Hermitage House (September 6, 1962), entitled "One of Tidewater's Oldest Homes." In 1955, Joseph and Edna Miriam Wallace purchased the house from James Collier. But in this 1962 article Mrs. Wallace was about to remarry and looking to sell Hermitage House. A picture of Mrs. Wallace was included as were several pictures of the house's features.
- Admiral John K. and Evelyn M. Beling purchased the house 1965. While Admiral Beling lived in this house he was the Commanding Officer on the USS Forrestal, and is best remembered for his heroic actions when a fire broke out on the ship on July 1967. See more about Admiral Beling in Chapter 8.
- In 1970 the Virginian Pilot did another feature of the house (February 15, 1970) "Even the Squeaks are Antiques at the Smiths Place" – this time with renters Lt Colonel and Mrs. Horton Smith. The article said the Belings still owned the house but were at that time stationed in D. C. This article as well as the article with Mrs. Wallace noted the fireplaces in the living and dining rooms that were believed to be hand carved with a pocketknife.
- In 1977 the Beling's sold the house to Michael and Mary Frances Wasteneys. The Beacon featured the house in an article (May 6, 1979) related to the Wasteneys opening the house to the public for a tour that would benefit the Virginia Beach Pops Symphony. The article mentioned the ancient black walnut trees on the grounds of the house that according to the current homeowners still produce nuts today. The Wasteneys said they delayed their landscaping plans, awaiting the completion of sewerage in the area. Instead they concentrated on restoration of the old floors, in which they

HISTORY OF THE THOROUGHGOOD NEIGHBORHOOD

spent at least three months on hands and knees removing layer upon layer of varnish and wax. Mrs. Wasteneys said on the window in the library nearest the fireplace, "J Ol" had been scratched on one of the panes – she said someone by the name of "Ewell" pointed it out when he came to see the house because he had once lived in it. Mr. Ewell said he'd been told that a girl who lived there had scratched it with the diamond in her engagement ring to see if the diamond was real. *Note: The senior Mr. A. E. Ewell died in 1950, so the Mr. Ewell Mrs. Wasteneys talked to was likely A. E. Ewell's son Joe Edwin Ewell, whose mother was the first Mrs. Ewell. As you will read in the Ewell section, the Ewells lived in the Hermitage House while awaiting their house to be built at 4124 Ewell Road - sometime after World War I.*

- In 2001 the Wasteneys sold the Hermitage House to John and Marianne Littel, who are the current homeowners. Mrs. Littel is a member of both the Princess Anne and Thoroughgood Garden Clubs. The Littels have done extensive renovations in an effort to be "good stewards of the house and property's history," according to Mr. Littel. The renovation was described in detail in an article in the Virginian Pilot (July 22, 2007). Although in 2001 the house was badly outdated, the Littels saw the potential with its heart-of-pine floors, wide crown molding, hand-carved fireplace mantels, and blown glass windowpanes. Renovation took six years, much of it undertaken by the Littels themselves. The couple even made a canvas floor cloth, similar to the one that currently is in the Adam Thoroughgood House. In an article in the Virginian Pilot ("Hermitage House – the other one – makes historic list," March 20, 2008) said the house had been approved for listing on the National Register of Historic Places.

Ewell Point. The only part of Ewell Road that was part of the original Collier tract was the north side of Ewell Road between Whitethorne and both sides of Stanfield. Ewell *Point* (i.e., Ewell Road past Stanfield Road) was not part of the original Thoroughgood tract the Colliers developed. However, in the 1966/67 Thoroughgood Civic League Constitution and By-laws the

NEIGHBORHOOD ANCHORS

"present residents of Ewell Point" were specifically included within the bounds of Thoroughgood and the Thoroughgood Civic League.

The primary developers of Ewell Point were the Ewells and the Nixons, and what a history those two families had.

First about the Ewells: Much of the following information comes from a charming hand-written history of Ewell Point by Catherine Nixon (since deceased), and an interview with Anne Greenberg (still living) – both daughters of Julian C. and Hazeltine Nixon. Ms. Nixon said Mr. Ewell's family owned and farmed the land around Ewell Point, and Mr. Ewell grew up there as a boy. His boyhood home is no longer standing but was located around the area of Wakefield Court. Their farm was called World's End Farm, so named when a man was making a delivery and the farm was difficult to locate.

As an adult, Mr. Ewell was a farmer initially – he supplied produce to the U.S. military and owned A. E. Ewell Lynnhaven Oysters. In those days, the oysters were much larger than they are today. There was a story in the book "Lower Tidewater Virginia" Volume 2, by Rogers Dey Wichard, Ph.D., in 1959 which discussed a famous oyster house. It was called O'Keefe's Casino located on the oceanfront directly in line with the brick train station at Cape Henry. President Howard Taft visited there in 1909. Prior to the President's visit, O'Keefe offered a prize for the prettiest barrel of oysters brought in by his regular oyster suppliers, which included "Tony" Ewell – as Mr. Ewell was known. Mr. Ewell oystered on the west side of the Lynnhaven River. In the end, Mr. O'Keefe had to call off the contest because all the oysters submitted by all his suppliers were "too beautiful." A picture of O'Keefe's Casino can be found on page 17 of Amy Waters Yarsinski's book "Lost Virginia Beach."

Later, Mr. Ewell's life would be dominated by politics. He was a member of the Virginia House of Delegates, representing Princess Anne County. The Virginia House of Delegates confirmed that an Arnold Edwin Ewell served as a member of the House from 1899–1901, and then again from 1920-1923. He was a Democrat. His 1923 House profile said he was born in Princess Anne County on July 20, 1875 and died June 8, 1950. He was a Methodist, and was educated by the Princess Anne County Public Schools, Randolph-Macon Academy, and Eastman's Business College. His House profile listed his occupation as a farmer and real estate developer. In the House of Delegates his committee assignments included Chesapeake and its Tributaries; Counties, Cities, and Towns; Retrenchment and the Economy;

HISTORY OF THE THOROUGHGOOD NEIGHBORHOOD

and Roads and Internal Navigation. A picture of Mr. Ewell and his three sisters, Mary, Nora, and Alexina is provided on page 96 in Stephen Mansfield's book "Princess Anne County and Virginia Beach, a pictorial history." Noting Mr. Ewell's participation in the House of Delegates, Dr. Mansfield says Mr. Ewell followed those terms with four years on the County Board of Supervisors. Mrs. Greenberg said Mr. Ewell was also the Game and Fisheries Commissioner in Kempsville. In a Google search, Mr. Ewell was listed in the 17th Annual Report of the Commission of Fisheries of Virginia (October 1, 1914 to September 30, 1915) representing Princess Anne. There is indication, however, he served longer than just those years. Mrs. Greenberg said Judge Benjamin Dey White, who owned nearby White Acre Farm, mentored Mr. Ewell's political life.

Back to Ms. Nixon's story – Before Mr. Ewell could build his house *(the large brown two-story home at 4124 Ewell Point)*; he had to first build Ewell "Lane" which was a private dirt road at the time. He brought in a sawmill to produce the lumber to build his house, the barns and other outbuildings. The lumber came from the area surrounding Ewell Point, according to Mrs. Greenberg. Mr. Ewell built a big barn. Mrs. Greenberg recalled that it was bigger than the brown house, and the barn loft was perfect for the dances that she and her brother held there occasionally when they were teenagers. The barn is no longer there, but was located on the right (south) side of the brown house. Mr. Ewell also built a potato barn that still stands at 4153 Ewell Point, a washhouse, a garage, chicken house, and a tenant house that still stands at 4184 Ewell Point. While the construction was going on Mr. Ewell lived at the Hermitage House down the road. The timing of building the large brown house is a bit of a question. The city lists the house being built in 1906, but Mrs. Greenberg and Ms. Nixon said it was built after World War I, around 1919. There might have been a smaller structure there in 1906, but not the present large brown house currently standing at 4124 Ewell Point.

Mrs. Greenberg said during (and prior to) the time of building the large brown house, Mr. Ewell was married to the first Mrs. Ewell (from Kempsville). Mrs. Greenberg never met the first Mrs. Ewell. Mr. Ewell and the first Mrs. Ewell had two children – a daughter, Virginia Ewell Whitehurst, and son Joe Edwin Ewell. After the Mrs. Ewell's death, Mr. Ewell met Miss Louise Hooper, a Latin teacher studying at the University of Richmond to be a social worker.

NEIGHBORHOOD ANCHORS

A. E. and Louise later married. Two old newspaper clippings recount the wedding. *(Note: There is no date or identification of the newspaper for the clippings, but a different newspaper article in the Virginia Beach Sun-News said the Ewells were married in 1924).* The wedding announcement noted that the Ewells were married in the home of Mrs. Ewell's cousin, Mr. and Mrs. Minton W. Talbot in Norfolk County. The article said the Hooper family was a direct descendant of William Hooper, one of the signers of the Declaration of Independence. *(Note: In 1975 after Mrs. Ewell moved to a nursing home, Rufus Cromwell, who managed the house for Mrs. Ewell's Trustee, found in the attic of 4124 Ewell Point, an original letter with waxed seal from William Hooper to Robert Smith, Merchant, Edenton, N.C. The letter advised that General Howe was receiving reinforcements, that thousands were flocking to General Washington, that Clinton with all his strength had arrived in Staten Island with 12,000 Hessians expected. Mr. Cromwell turned the original letter over to the Trustee, and later gave a copy of the letter to Anne. According to Mrs. Greenberg's daughter, an online search showed that Mrs. Ewell's grandson sold the letter several years ago for $64,000.)* The wedding announcement also said the bride's maternal great grandfather was a descendant of Sir Christopher Gale, who with William Byrd settled the boundary line between North Carolina and Virginia. The wedding announcement said Mr. and Mrs. Ewell would settle in Mr. Ewell's "World's End Farm" in *Lynnhaven*, Virginia. Mrs. Greenberg recalled that before the mailing address was Virginia Beach, Virginia, this area's mailing address was Bayside, Virginia, and prior to that, was Lynnhaven, Virginia.

Like Mr. Ewell, the second Mrs. Ewell was quite accomplished. She obtained a Bachelor of Arts Degree from Sweet Briar College, where she was president of her class for four years. According to the Sweet Briar College website, Mrs. Ewell was noted as one of the first five graduates of Sweet Briar College, class of 1910. She was named an outstanding Alumna Award Recipient in 1968. She worked in the Navy Department during World War I in Washington and at the close of the war enlisted in the Red Cross Home Service Work. Three years prior to marrying Mr. Ewell, Mrs. Ewell was a Red Cross Field Representative in forty-nine counties in Virginia, and during this time she also enrolled in the University of Richmond to obtain a certificate to pursue social work. After marrying Mr. Ewell, Mrs. Ewell organized and was the first president of the Princess Anne Woman's Club. As noted in

HISTORY OF THE THOROUGHGOOD NEIGHBORHOOD

Stephen Mansfield's book, "Princess Anne County and Virginia Beach, a pictorial history" during the summer of 1925, the Home Demonstration Club of Kempsville resolved to reorganize as the Women's Club of Princess Anne County. Dr. Mansfield wrote that with Mrs. A. E. Ewell as its first president, the membership reached 150 the first year and the club began a range of cultural activities that led to the formation of separate book, drama, music, and garden clubs. Mrs. Ewell became a social worker in Norfolk, and (without success) worked to build a high school for black children in Princess Anne County, since at that time there was not one. For her Master's Thesis, Mrs. Ewell wrote the book "Children Committed to the State Department of Public Welfare by the Juvenile Court of Norfolk, Virginia: A Study of Eighty-five Children Committed January 1, 1927-December 31, 1936." It was 188 pages long and printed by the College of William and Mary in 1938.

Ms. Nixon said Mrs. Ewell was largely responsible for raising money for the people of Princess Anne County to build the Tidewater Victory Memorial Hospital. This hospital for tuberculosis patients opened in 1937 in the same building that now houses Willis Furniture. Mrs. Ewell's father died of tuberculosis, and her brother also had tuberculosis, which may have provided her drive and determination to see this hospital built. Note: the Virginian Pilot ran an article on March 15, 2010, "What's in a name? Wayside Village Shoppes" which talked about the hospital. A 1937 photograph of the old hospital site is also provided in the book "Princess Anne County and Virginia Beach, a pictorial history," which also noted that Mrs. A. E. Ewell of Princess Anne County headed the formation of the Tidewater Tuberculosis Hospital Association as it raised funds and selected a site near Thalia Creek on Virginia Beach Boulevard.

Mrs. Ewell was named as Princess Anne's Woman of Outstanding Accomplishment for 1953 as noted in the Virginia Beach Sun-News in an article (March 11, 1954). A special committee named by the Princess Anne County Business and Professional Women's Club made the selection, and the award was presented by the Norfolk Public Affairs Chairman of the Virginia Federation of Business and Professional Women's Clubs. The citation noted Mrs. Ewell's unselfish and distinguished service to humanity through her extensive welfare and social service work, and through all phases of Civic betterment thus greatly improving the cultural, educational and social life of the community, the State, and the Nation. The citation noted that during

NEIGHBORHOOD ANCHORS

her entire life, Mrs. Ewell had been especially interested in underprivileged persons, having done outstanding work in health and welfare programs.

Mrs. Greenberg said in the crash of 1929 and the Great Depression Mr. Ewell lost much of his real estate holdings. At the time he owned land at Chesapeake Beach. However he did not lose his house at 4124 Ewell Point, or that surrounding land, which he later began to sub-divide and sell off. In 1943 Julian Nixon purchased 65 acres on the right (south) side of Ewell Point, and he and his family inhabited the Potato Barn. At the time of the sale, the Nixon property was described as being at the intersection of land owned by Ewell, Frizzell, and White. Henry Keeling bought seven acres on the left (north) side of Ewell Point in 1944 and remodeled the tenant house. At the time of the sale, the Keeling land was described as being bounded to the north by land owned by John Daley.

Ms. Nixon noted that the Mr. Ewell's only son Arnold (with second wife Louise) was killed in the Normandy invasion on D-Day. He was 19 years old. That was a very sad time for the Ewells. Soon after, the Ewells were surprised to learn that son Arnold had married Florence Yinger prior to being sent overseas by the Navy, and she was pregnant with their grandson, named Arnold Edwin ("Tony") Ewell II, born in 1945.

Mr. Ewell's obituary in the Virginian Pilot (June 9, 1950) said for more than half a century he played a leading role in the development of Princess Anne County, and particularly in the development of Chesapeake Beach, much of the territory having been in his family for many years. In addition to his accomplishments already noted above, he was a member of the original planning committee that played a large part in the construction of the first paved road from Norfolk to Virginia Beach. He was a former President of the Norfolk Truckers Exchange, and served on the School Board and Red Cross. He was (at that time) the oldest living member of Haygood Methodist Church and had served various positions during his membership of 50 years, including a member of the Board of Stewards and Trustee. He was 76 when he died.

After Mr. Ewell died in 1950, Mrs. Ewell turned the large brown house (4124 Ewell Point) into four apartments and built two guest cottages on either side of the house in order to have sufficient income on which to live. The earliest Civic League records show Mrs. Ewell's address as "20" Ewell Point in 1959. This same 1959 Thoroughgood directory showed others living

HISTORY OF THE THOROUGHGOOD NEIGHBORHOOD

at 20 Ewell Point – as related to the apartments Louise created out of the house. The tenants at that time were John and Joan Grahm, Lawrence and Alene McEntee, Walter and Louise Luffsey, and Paul and Laura Gerisch. Mrs. Ewell was still living at 4124 Ewell Point in 1970, as listed in that year's Thoroughgood Civic League Directory. Mrs. Ewell later moved to the Lafayette Villa nursing home in Norfolk, where she died in August 24, 1976. Her obituary reported she was a native of Edenton, N. C., the daughter of the late Henry DeBerniere Hooper and Mrs. Jessie Wright Hooper, and was a member of Old Donation Episcopal Church. The obituary said after her husband's death, she entered what then was Richmond Professional Institute (now Virginia Commonwealth University), earned her master's degree, and worked with the Social Service Bureau in Norfolk. The obituary also said she helped to form the Princess Anne Historical Society. She was 86 when she died. *(Note: There is confusion on the point of when she worked on her master's – Mrs. Greenberg said she believes it was not after her husband's death, but while he was alive. She believes prior to a fire in the house, there were letters in the attic from Mr. Ewell and son Arnold to Mrs. Ewell while she was studying for her master's degree in Richmond. Also the book she wrote for her master's thesis was published in 1938, and Mr. Ewell died in 1950.)*

The Nixons. According to the Haygood United Methodist Church (HUMC) website, Hazeltine Nixon was married to Julian C. Nixon. They had four children: Mary Catherine (Catherine) Nixon; William M. (Billy) Nixon; Julian Harris Nixon; and Anne Nixon (later Anne Greenberg). In 1942, Hazeltine Nixon was treated for tuberculosis at the Tidewater Victory Memorial Hospital, located on the current site of Willis Furniture. Mrs. Greenberg said it was just a coincidence that her mother was treated in the same hospital that Mrs. Ewell helped to create. The Ewells and the Nixons hadn't met yet, but would soon. To aide in her recovery Mrs. Nixon's doctor suggested she needed a restful and quiet setting so Julian, who was in real estate and living in Ocean View (in Norfolk) at the time, purchased the A. Ewell farm (i.e., World's End Farm) at the end of Ewell Road on the Western Branch Lynnhaven River and moved the family there from Norfolk. The HUMC article said that while in the hospital Hazeltine Nixon promised God that if she recovered she would dedicate the rest of her life to Him, so when they moved to World's End Farm, they joined Haygood United Methodist Church on December 5, 1943 and became very active members. Both

NEIGHBORHOOD ANCHORS

Hazeltine Nixon and daughter Catherine sang in the church choir. Daughter Anne was choir director for a year, and when needed, served as church organist. Many of the "long time" church members remember enjoying church picnics and attending church meetings on their beautiful property, which is still in the family. Hazeltine Nixon died January 25, 1976 at age 87. Mrs. Nixon had a church circle named after her, there is a pew dedicated to the family in the main sanctuary, and one of the beautiful stained glass windows is dedicated to her and her husband. Hazeltine Nixon's obituary says she was also a member of the World Literacy Prayer Group, and the Virginia Beach Republican Women's Club.

Catherine Nixon said in 1955 when the Thoroughgood and Hermitage farms were joined and developed, roads cut into Ewell "Lane." Catherine Nixon's father, Julian C. Nixon dedicated the private "lane" to Princess Anne County. It was widened and paved. Mr. Nixon passed away on April 19, 1977 at age 89. His obituary said he was a retired realtor and former state committeeman of the Republican Party. He was also the former president of the Southwark Hunt Club and an organizer of the Ocean View Civic League.

Brother Julian Harris Nixon died August 10, 1995 at age 81. His residence at the time of his death was listed as the 4100 block of Ewell Road. His obituary said he was a retired teacher and researcher at Columbia University, and graduated from the College of William and Mary in 1936, and was a U.S. Army veteran of World War II. Brother William M. Nixon passed away around July 9, 2004. Daughter Catherine Nixon continued to live in the Potato Barn, and was known by neighbors as a wonderful person with a love of the history on Ewell Point. She passed away in 2005.

Mrs. Greenberg went away to school, married, and lived in New York City with her husband and four children. She was away from Thoroughgood for much of the time between 1947 and 1976, and therefore missed the major part of the neighborhood's development. She recalled growing up on Ewell Point as a child, and said her father purchased 65 acres on the right (south) side of Ewell Road to Stanfield Road in 1943. The Nixons were not farmers, but rented out part of the land to the Yoder Family, who farmed the land. Mr. Meier purchased two parcels of land from Mr. Nixon – on one parcel he built a home that subsequently burned and on another parcel he used as a plant nursery. Mrs. Greenberg said her father owned the old Ewell house - not the brown house at 4124 Ewell Point, but rather the boyhood

HISTORY OF THE THOROUGHGOOD NEIGHBORHOOD

home of A. E. Ewell that used to stand around the area of Wakefield Court. He wanted to renovate it, however, he could not get electricity extended there, so they lived in the Potato Barn instead.

Mrs. Greenberg recalled as a child making evening walks up Ewell Road – how lovely the tunnel of trees were on Ewell Road between what is now Dunstan Lane and Whitethorne Road – particularly with the fire flies lighting the way. She said they picked up their mail in a mail cluster on "Route 1" as they called it (i.e., today's Independence Boulevard). She attended high school at Granby High School in Norfolk, since the only other school in the area (Kempsville) had just eleven grades, making entrance to her college of choice difficult. She rode each day to Granby High School with Mr. Ewell and her father (who both had offices in the Monticello Arcade in downtown Norfolk), and Mrs. Ewell, who did social work in downtown Norfolk. To get there (before I-64 and the major roads of today), they went by way of Robbins Corner to Shell Road (which used to be much longer). It must have taken a long time. Mrs. Greenberg said she was tardy a lot. She would be dropped off at Granby High School in the morning but then took the trolley to downtown after school and did homework awaiting the ride home. Such a "car pool" was necessary in those days to share in gas rationing during the war. Anne graduated from Granby in 1947, and went away to college. She met her future husband, David Greenberg, when she went to New York City in 1958. They lived in New York's Staten Island from 1961 – 1975. Anne and David Greenberg returned to Ewell Point and purchased the large brown house in 1975. They are listed in the 1978 Thoroughgood Civic League Directory at 4124 Ewell Point.

Historic properties on Ewell Point:

- **Ewell House**. Located at 4124 Ewell Point this large two-story brown-shingled house was the family home for Mrs. and Mrs. A. E. Ewell. According to city records the house was constructed in 1906, but the present structure of 15 finished rooms including four bedrooms thought to have been constructed after World War I ended. The original address for this house was World's End Farm, and later it was changed to 20 Ewell Point. David and Anne Greenberg later purchased the house. Anne Greenberg is the daughter of Julian and Hazeltine Nixon. Mrs. Greenberg lives there today.
- **Potato Barn**. Located at 4153 Ewell Point, this small red house was

NEIGHBORHOOD ANCHORS

built by Mr. Ewell and used as a barn to store potatoes when the area was farmland. It is one of the few homes in Thoroughgood with a basement. This house became the primary and long-term residence of Julian and Hazeltine Nixon, and Anne Greenberg's daughter still lives there. City records indicate this home site is platted as Thoroughgood "Shores." In the 1959 and 1961 Thoroughgood Civic League Directory, the address was listed as 9 Ewell Point. Julian and Hazeltine Nixon lived there then, as well as in 1969 and 1970, when the directory changed the address to 4153 Ewell Road. By the time the next available directory (1978) was printed both Mr. and Mrs. Nixon had passed away and their son Julian H. and daughter Catherine were listed as living at 4153 Ewell Point.

- **_Tenant House_**. Located at 4184 Ewell Point, this rambling one-story adorable red wood framed house was built by Mr. Ewell. Ms. Nixon called it the "tenant" house, but the present owners (Sue and Tom McGeorge) heard it was also called the "cook's" cottage because Mr. and Mrs. Ewell's cook lived there when it was a one-room house. City records show the follow-on owners were Henry T. and Clarissa Keeling. Mrs. McGeorge said that Mr. Keeling attempted to renovate the house in the 1940s, but couldn't buy renovation materials until after the war. He then expanded the house, and kept a scrapbook of the renovation process. Mrs. McGeorge said Mr. Keeling used to bird hunt, but when his beloved bird dog was killed in the construction, he sold the property. Mr. Keeling moved to the area between Dunstan Lane and Ewell Road, east of Wakefield Drive, at 4183 White Acre Road, according to the 1992 Thoroughgood Civic League Directory. If you look at the "Whiteacre" neighborhood plat (i.e., White Acres Road and Court), Mr. Keeling's property is north of that plat. At that time the land was not as developed as it is now and provided room for his bird dogs to roam. The city's land records indicate the Tenant House was sold to Cosmo Corporation in August 1955, who held it for about three months, then sold it to Joseph T. and Mary L. McDonald in November 1955. Mr. McDonald was part of the Langley and McDonald Engineering Firm. In the 1959 and 1961 Thoroughgood Civic League Directory, the address was 2 Ewell Point Road, but by the 1969 directory it had changed to

HISTORY OF THE THOROUGHGOOD NEIGHBORHOOD

4184 Ewell Road. Mrs. McDonald used the house for tea parties, and it was at that time the house was featured in an antiques magazine. The McDonald's sold the property to Perry R. and Agnes D. Chambers in 1980, and the name changed to Perry R. and *Sherry R.* Chambers in 1986. The McGeorge's bought it from the Chambers in 1992, and live there currently.

- **_Ewell Cottage #1._** In 1969 Mrs. Ewell sub-divided her large lot. Howard and Suzanne Horton jumped at the chance to sell their then much nicer new brick home in Lake Smith Terrace to buy one of Mrs. Ewell's rental cottages at 4112 Ewell Road on the north side of the large brown house for $25,000. At this point the cottage was old, run down, and small. Over time, the Horton's turned the small guest cottage at the end of Ewell Point into a spacious, lovely home with a beautiful view of Ewell Cove. When he was 16 years old, Howard Horton recalled his parents (Gurnie and Ethel Horton) purchased a waterfront lot at 4140 Ewell Road (or 14 Ewell Road as it was known back then) from Henry Keeling in 1955/56, and Howard helped his father (a building contractor) build their house. The Horton family previously lived in the Norview section of Norfolk. Howard initially went to Norview High School – so did Suzanne Horton. In fact, one of Suzanne Horton's teachers was another longtime Thoroughgood resident, Lois Wootton. Howard Horton's family was in the construction business and built several of the houses on Ewell Point, and several of the Horton's family members live in various houses on Ewell Point today. Howard Horton recalls a few things about Mrs. Ewell. One thing was she used to have lots of bushes and shrubbery around her house – so much so that he could hardly see the big brown house and rental cottages from his parents house. He recalls that Mrs. Ewell was a task master – she would hire young boys to do the yard work and then sit a kitchen chair in the yard while they were working with a wind up clock in her lap to time their work. Howard Horton recalled seeing Mrs. Ewell driving her light green 1955 Ford past his yard on many occasions, and noted she was a fast driver for her age. *(Note: Anne Greenberg recalled that Mrs. Ewell once told her that she was one of the first women to drive a car. Anne Greenberg assumed it was in*

NEIGHBORHOOD ANCHORS

connection with World War I or her Red Cross work.) It's funny that even after the Horton's bought the cottage, Mrs. Ewell's detached garage remained on the Horton's lot, and Mrs. Ewell continued to park her 1955 Ford in what is now the Horton's garage until she stopped driving a number of years past 1969.

- **_Ewell Cottage #2_**. Mr. and Mrs. Olds bought the second cottage. They demolished it and built a brick ranch. The address is now 4125 Ewell Road.
- **_Thoroughgood Shores_**. City records indicate approximately six home sites on Ewell Road south of Stanfield was once owned by Julian and Hazeltine Nixon, and when the Nixons developed the property in January/February 1965 they recorded the sub-division for those plats as Thoroughgood "Shores" according to city records (Map Book 64, page 44 and Map Book 65, page 55).

CHAPTER 3

The Sixties

Expansion of Thoroughgood. The 1960s saw the expansion of Thoroughgood into the following sections – all developed by Charles Bowden. As in the last chapter, the map book and page number is provided for those wanting to review the plat books at the Virginia Beach Municipal Center.

- Section 7 (July 1965, Map Book 66, page 38) included six lots on the south side of Ewell Road from the turn at Whitethorne Road to Wakefield Drive.
- Section 8, Part 1 (December 1966, Map Book 71, page 9) included four lots on the south side of Ewell Road past Wakefield Drive.
- Section 8, Part 2 (July 1966, Map Book 75, page 50) included both sides of Delray Drive between Ewell Road and Wakefield Drive.

Charles Bowden would eventually build houses on Whitethorne Road, Westwell Lane, Chandler Lane, Ewell Road, Delray Drive, Wakefield Drive, and Pecan Grove Road, according to his widow Jean. He had a reputation for quality, and often had repeat business from homeowners. An example was the house Mr. Bowden built for Farm Fresh Grocery Store owner Gene Walters on Delray Drive (where Bob Coffey lives today), and then another home in Great Neck when Gene Walters moved there. Bob Coffey said years later Mr. Bowden came by to see if everything was still okay with the home he built on Delray. Mr. Bowden died on March 4, 2010.

Thoroughgood Shores? As noted in chapter 2, the Virginia Beach plat books indicate a few houses in Thoroughgood labeled as Thoroughgood "Shores." These properties are currently (as of 2012) listed in the

HISTORY OF THE THOROUGHGOOD NEIGHBORHOOD

Thoroughgood Shores subdivision according to city records and developed by Julian and Hazeltine Nixon.

- January 1965, Map Book 64, page 44 shows lot 6 on the south side of Ewell Road where the road intersects with Stanfield Road.
- February 1965, Map Book 65, page 55 shows lots 2, 3, 4, 5, and 7 on the south side of Ewell Road where the road intersects with Stanfield Road.
- Lot 1, developed in June 1964 is not labeled Thoroughgood Shores – instead it is labeled "Lot 1 – Nixon tract."

Thoroughgood Estates began in the 1960s? Thoroughgood Estates was difficult to research. It has always been advertised as being developed in the late 1970s, and often described as bounded by Ewell Road, Independence, Dunstan Lane, and Wakefield Drive. Certainly that is true for the newer part – but Thoroughgood Estates is much bigger than that. As adopted January 15, 1968, the Thoroughgood Civic League Constitution and By-laws were amended to include "that portion of the Frizzell Farm bounded north of Bayside Road (i.e., Independence Boulevard) and west of Ewell Road." After pouring over old plat books at the Municipal Center, Thoroughgood Estates was found to have several major sections, and the two below were developed in the 1960s. These areas are what the Constitution and By-laws were amended to include. While Thoroughgood Civic League Directories were not available for every year, the 1969 directory shows homeowners living on Keeler Lane, Biscayne Drive, and Rust Drive, and the 1970 directory showed homeowners on Independence Boulevard. Thoroughgood Estates, Inc. developed both sections below:

- Section 1 (August 1961, Map Book 55, page 11) is the area bounded by the north sides of Keeler Lane/Biscayne Drive, and both sides of Delray Drive (from Biscayne Drive to Ewell Road), and then Ewell Road (from Delray Drive to Keeler Lane).
- Section 2 (November 1962, Map Book 57, page 34) is the area between Keeler Lane and Independence Boulevard (on both sides of Five Forks Road), starting at Ewell Road and ending at Gracetown.

For the above early Thoroughgood Estates sites, the Thoroughgood Civic League was vocal in 1963 with the Virginia Beach Planning Commission to oppose lowering the zoning for lots from RS-2 (30,000 Square Feet) to RS-3 (20,000 SF).

THE SIXTIES

Rudacil Land. The 1960s saw the development of the south side of Wakefield Court and adjoining corner of Wakefield Drive. The neighborhood plat for this development does not refer to Thoroughgood, but just simply the Bayside Borough. Regardless, they are decidedly part of Thoroughgood. There were three lots developed – 4213 and 4209 Wakefield Court, and 1468 Wakefield Drive. Coite B. and Clarice G. Rudacil owned them. According to Frank and Lois Wootton who live at 1468 Wakefield Drive, their land marked the end of Wakefield Drive at the time it was developed in 1970. The Woottons said Wakefield Drive in front of their lot was a dirt road that they had to fill in with gravel in order to get Virginia Power to bring electricity to their house.

Mrs. C.B. Rudacil was on the membership and attendance committee of the 1959 Thoroughgood Civic League. Also at that time Coite B. and Clarice Rudacil were listed as living at 2414 Thoroughgood Drive. That house numbering would have changed in the 1960s, but it is unclear what their house number would have changed to since the Rudacil's were not listed in the next available directory.

Adam Thoroughgood House. On April 9, 1960 there was a formal "Presentation of the 17th Century Garden of the Adam Thoroughgood House." The several-page brochure is in the archives of Virginia Wesleyan College, Henry Clay Hofheimer II Library, and also available through the Sergeant Memorial Collection inside the Pretlow Anchor Branch Library in Norfolk. The brochure provided a layout of the gardens. The gardens were a gift of The Garden Club of Virginia. Alden Hopkins designed the gardens.

In other news, according to the Norfolk Museum Bulletin in 1961 as recounted in the book "Bayside History Trail," the Adam Thoroughgood House property was given to the City of Norfolk by the Adam Thoroughgood House Foundation on March 21, 1961. The City of Norfolk assigned the Chrysler Museum to manage the house. It was noted in the City of Virginia Beach, Community Legislative Agenda, 2008 General Assembly Session that the Adam Thoroughgood House Foundation dissolved in the early 1960s after the property was deeded to Norfolk (Deed Book 676, page 523).

Front Entrance – 14 Years of Controversy. This was likely the biggest and longest-lasting controversy in our neighborhood's history. It was highly emotional. It will be discussed in this and the next two chapters. This recounting is based on Civic League notes and many, many newspaper articles

HISTORY OF THE THOROUGHGOOD NEIGHBORHOOD

on this subject. Although every effort was made to be impartial and tell the story as recounted mostly in (what would hope to be unbiased) newspaper articles, it was newspaper articles retained in Civic League records, so there is no telling whether all articles (pro and con) were kept, nor if the "whole" story is being told.

First, let's be clear about the area being discussed. The front entrance as used in this discussion refers to the main/original entrance to the neighborhood off Pleasure House Road. It includes Thoroughgood Square, the area (currently) occupied by both Thoroughgood and Church Point Commons shopping centers, and the land behind it that extends to Collier Lane. This area was originally mostly woodland, with the exception of the sales office at the end of Thoroughgood Square. Home sites did not begin until past Collier Lane. The area comprised about 12 acres. At the time, large brick columns existed to announce the entrance. There was a white picket fence on either side extending to the C&P Building on the right, and the present day First Court Road on the left. There was no Thoroughgood or Church Point Commons. Some residents at the time expected the entrance to stay this way forever – because they said that was what they were told when the first purchased the property. However, this was not to be.

The year was 1969, and Brigadier General Austin Brunelli (USMC Retired) was the president of the Thoroughgood Civic League. Danny and Richard Collier had taken over the duties of Thoroughgood development, and were both in their mid-20s at the time. The Thoroughgood Civic League sent a notification to the membership to advise that Thorogood Corporation planned to build a shopping center on Parcel A, Section 1 of Thoroughgood and adjoining parcels on either side, and in back of Thoroughgood Square. The area had been zoned for limited commercial development since 1955. Thorogood Corporation explained that the 'shopping center' in question was really 15 Colonial styled professional office buildings and small specialty shops, keeping in mind the "prestige" of Thoroughgood. Regardless, the Civic League was concerned with the effect a shopping center would have on traffic congestion, the safety hazard posed for the children attending Hermitage Elementary School, the resulting change to the image of the entrance, and the destruction of natural woodland areas. That led to a firestorm of newspaper articles on the issue. The representatives of the residents of Thoroughgood presented a petition of nearly 1,000 individual signatures

THE SIXTIES

to City Council of Virginia Beach to request a public hearing before the Planning Commission on the subject, and to ask the commission to rezone the property to recreational or residential.

Thoroughgood Civic League hired the attorney Morris Fine to represent the residents, and created a committee to assist the Civic League in preparing for this battle. The committee was comprised of William Russell, Chairman, and members Henry Pezella, Donald Holland, William Colden, Albert Arsenault, and Richard Lindell. That group, along with several hundred Thoroughgood residents descended upon a City Council meeting on February 10, 1969. The residents filled the chamber hall, lined the stairwells, and spilled out into the hall below. Some residents had to stand outside the building during a windy, cold afternoon. Inside, Morris Fine asked the city for the aforementioned rezoning, and then the residents were given time to speak. Many of the residents said they had been led to believe that property would remain vacant to serve as a buffer between the neighborhood and commercial development, although there was nothing in writing. The Mayor had to use his gavel liberally to maintain order amongst what was often irate speeches followed by wild applause. The City Attorney said rezoning the land without the application of the owner would open the door to a costly lawsuit he thought the city would lose. Nevertheless, Planning Director Patrick L. Standing and Bayside Councilman Larry Marshall were directed to give council a recommendation at its February 24th meeting.

Thoroughgood Civic League called a special meeting of the membership on February 17, 1969 to go over all actions taken and to discuss future plans. One of the suggestions was to send letters to city officials. On February 18, 1969, President Brunelli initiated a letter-writing campaign to the Mayor and City Council to formally state the resident's resolution. In these letters, he recounted the request to rezone to residential. The resolution specifically said it requested rezoning to single dwellings the same size, style and construction consistent with other residences in Thoroughgood. At the same time, officials of Thorogood Corporation presented City Council with the plans for commercial development, and assured Council it would be an asset to Thoroughgood. On February 21, 1969, Thorogood Corporation filed an application for a building permit to build a 1½-story building of Colonial design to house a bookshop and the shop of an interior decorator.

In preparation for the February 24th council meeting, and in anticipation of

◄ **HISTORY OF THE THOROUGHGOOD NEIGHBORHOOD**

another barrage of attendees, Mayor Dusch sent a letter to the Thoroughgood Civic League to instruct them to warn residents that due to the fire hazard created at the last meeting, no overcrowding of future meetings would be tolerated. There would only be about 50 seats available in the courtroom where council would meet. They would be filled on a first-come, first-served basis. Fire marshals would be on site to ensure all fire regulations were strictly enforced.

In the February 24th council meeting, residents complied with space limitations, but took up every available space. Councilman Marshall, a Thoroughgood resident, said he found no evidence to indicate Thorogood Corporation had ever tried to mislead the residents or acted in bad faith concerning its plans for the property, and restated that if City Council changed the zoning, it would leave itself open to a court fight on the matter. Regardless, council conceded to directing the Planning Commission to conduct a public hearing on April 8, 1969 aimed at revoking "limited commercial" zoning on 12 acres at the neighborhood entrance. The Planning Commission would then report its recommendation to City Council on April 28, 1969.

On February 26, 1969, the president and treasurer of the Thoroughgood Civic League signed the legal papers for Morris Fine to ask the Circuit Court for an injunction to restrain the Building Inspector from issuing a building permit to the Thorogood Corporation, and further restrain the Thorogood Corporation from constructing the building until the Planning Board hearings were held and final decision was rendered by the City Council. The injunction was granted. The Civic League sent this information to the membership in order to raise funds to continue on with this campaign. At least $10.00 was requested from each homeowner. Donations would be kept in a separate account, reported separately, and balance returned pro-rata once the issue was resolved.

Thoroughgood citizens then got to work in preparation for the Planning Commission, to include a traffic survey for Pleasure House Road, a statement from the Parent-Teacher Organization of Hermitage Elementary School that would be favorable to the neighborhood's position, and maps and aerial footage of the area in question both from 1955 and as it currently existed. There was a lot of research and preparation by many residents. Also a petition was sent to City Council from the Cape Henry Bird Club, who was against the shopping center in that it (they contended) would destroy a large

THE SIXTIES

rookery of herons and egrets near the entrance of the development. Then the Civic League sent a reminder to the residents about the upcoming Planning Meeting, inviting all to attend, even arranging for professional babysitting to be available. The Civic League provided the name and addresses for the members of the Planning Commission and urged the residents to send them a letter with their thoughts.

At the April 8th meeting, Thoroughgood residents once again packed the Council Chamber. The attorney for the residents again asked for rezoning, arguing when it was originally zoned commercial in 1955 there were very little shopping facilities, but there were plenty in present-day 1969, and more were not necessary. Mr. Fine brought up the heron/egret issue, and the traffic issue. The attorney for Thorogood Corporation said Independence Boulevard (which at the time was under construction) would alleviate the current traffic problems on Pleasure House Road, and pointed out there was already a commercial building on the site (i.e., the old sales office). Mr. Standing noted the commission had the letter from the Thorogood Corporation from 1955 stating the 12 acres would be used for commercial use. Mr. Standing acknowledged the existing building and noted there had been no objections over that building from the residents. Instead he felt the issue was a design problem – not a zoning problem, which he thought Thoroughgood residents would agree. This resulted in a roar of disagreement from the audience. At this point, over the objections of the residents, the Planning Commission decided to delay a decision on the matter by 30 days, in order to allow Mr. Standing time to attempt to work out a compromise.

The next hearing of the Planning Commission was May 13, 1969, and again notification was sent to residents to encourage them to attend. The commission deferred its decision when the Civic League asked for a postponement in order to present Standing's plan to their membership. On May 21, 1969, Director of Planning, Mr. Standing met directly with Thoroughgood residents and Thorogood Corporation at Bayside Presbyterian Church to make public his compromise proposal. The plan was to leave the entrance zoned commercial, but change one strip of land 150 feet on the west side of Collier Lane from commercial to residential. The proposal would also include a new entrance to Thoroughgood, which would be made by extending Hermitage Road to Pleasure House Road. It would also close Collier Lane to through traffic. This was referred to as the "Standing Plan."

◄ HISTORY OF THE THOROUGHGOOD NEIGHBORHOOD

Thoroughgood residents met on June 2, 1969, and by majority agreed to the Standing Plan, provided that Thorogood Corporation also agreed to the plan, would ensure the new entrance to be architecturally similar to the present entrance (estimated to cost $14,000) and be completed prior to any commercial property being built, and that the property facing Collier Road be rezoned RS-2.

On June 30, 1969 attorneys and officers for the Thoroughgood Civic League appeared before City Council in informal session to air their views regarding the matter.

The Planning Commission then met on June 10, 1969. By that time Bailey Condrey was the president of Thoroughgood Civic League. The residents voiced their approval of the plan with stipulations (noted above), however the Thorogood Corporation said they would not voluntarily agree to the Standing Plan, saying it was too complicated and too expensive. The residents then withdrew their approval, reverting back to the original request to make the entire property residential. The commission moved to have the property fronting Collier Lane rezoned to residential, which was seconded and adopted. Both Thorogood Corporation and the Thoroughgood residents threatened court action.

Next the City Council took up the issue in their general meeting of July 14, 1969, and dealt the final blow by refusing to adopt the Standing Plan. City Council said they had no right to change the zoning. This meant Thorogood Corporation won the battle to retain "limited commercial" zoning for the entire 12 acres at the entrance. Thoroughgood residents who had packed the City Council meeting hissed at the opponent, applauded their lawyer, and then fell silent when Councilman Marshall said he had received several "vulgar and abusive" telephone calls during the eight-month controversy, and that nothing in his seven years on the council had caused him so much concern.

In deciding the next step for the Civic League, Louis Fine (attorney for Thoroughgood residents) explained there was no statutory provision for an appeal of a zoning matter, per se. The City Council would have to be found as taking action that was arbitrary, capricious, or fraudulent, but given the Planning Commission's study there might be consideration given, and there was no evidence of that. And, attorney fees to pursue the matter could run as high as $5,000. After discussion, the Civic League Board decided

THE SIXTIES

to recommend no further action be taken. It also recommended that the balance remaining in the special Civic League account (collected for this issue) be left there in the event of future legal activities confronting the Civic League. At the general meeting on September 15, 1969 the recommendations of the Board were accepted.

See the next chapter for the continuation of this issue.

Last of the Lingering Hope for a Country Club. As previously mentioned, James Collier originally planned to build a country club in the plat section of Thoroughgood identified as Parcel A, at the end of Country Club Circle adjacent to the Adam Thoroughgood House. It would be near the boat ramp that was originally built for the neighborhood in Parcel B (across from Country Club Circle nearest the Lynnhaven River.) Plans for the country club were thwarted upon Collier's untimely death in 1957. Civic League minutes noted that the IRS would only allow the Thorogood Corporation to sell remaining home sites. In researching the notes following those years, the idea of a country club lived on with the Civic League, however. It received consideration by the Board in 1966 and 1967.

It gained more serious momentum when the Civic League Board proposed an alternative idea to the membership in their general meeting on March 27, 1968. The idea was to build a clubhouse (vice country club) suitable for meetings, informal social functions, etc., including swimming and wading pools, barbeque area, storage shed, badminton and tennis courts, and parking area and bicycle rack. The membership was asked their preference for locations: Country Club Circle, Ewell Road near the Church, or Shore Drive adjacent to Baylake Pines. It would cost a total of $150,000 and could be ready by the summer of 1968. Financing would require approximately 700 families in Thoroughgood and Thoroughgood Estates to purchase $400 in stock for the construction, followed by paying annual dues to cover upkeep, lifeguards, and such. Perhaps this was a sizeable investment, and admittedly many Thoroughgood homes had swimming pools already. Also, we had never had that many families as members of the Civic League, let alone invest in a club/swimming complex. To widen the pool of families, the membership was asked if they would consider extending membership to the clubhouse to Lake Smith Terrace and/or Baylake Pines. Questionnaires given to the membership were to be mailed to the "Country Club Committee." It is not known what the membership reaction was, but clearly this alternative (or

HISTORY OF THE THOROUGHGOOD NEIGHBORHOOD

any other) was not adopted. It was essentially the last chatter heard about the "country club." As a postscript, however, in 1988/89 the Pembroke Meadows neighborhood pool opened membership to Thoroughgood residents.

Post Office Mail Delivery. The January 16, 1968 general meeting passed a motion that the Civic League petition the Post Office Department for door to door mail delivery. One longtime resident thought that motion referred to asking the post office to allow the mailboxes in Thoroughgood to be affixed to the outside of the house, rather than curb-side. This was not an unreasonable request, since some of the houses in neighboring Lake Smith Terrace are grandfathered such that as long as the homeowners had house mailboxes when they first purchased their property, they can continue to use them – even today.

One thing that appears to have happened in the 1960s was the re-numbering of some of the houses in Thoroughgood. It appeared to occur on many streets – Arrowhead Point, Hermitage Point, Ewell Road, Bradston Road, Wakefield Drive, and Two Woods Road among others. One longtime resident thinks that was as a result of changing from an address of "Bayside, Virginia" to "Virginia Beach, Virginia" when the town of Virginia Beach merged with Princess Anne County in 1963.

As a coincidence, the use of Zoning Improvement Plan (ZIP) codes began July 1963, according to "The United States Postal Service, An American History (1775-2006)."

City Water Comes to Thoroughgood. Virginia Beach began buying water from Norfolk in 1925, but most Princess Anne County residents still used wells. Bringing city water into Thoroughgood was always a top priority of the Civic League, and they actively campaigned the city for it. In November 1967, the City of Virginia Beach notified Thoroughgood Civic League that the first section of the water main in Thoroughgood had been completed and tested. The City of Norfolk would need to chlorinate the system. A contract for the second (and final) half had been awarded and work started. After water became available, each homeowner was required to pay Virginia Beach a front footage fee (minimum of $400.00). The fee was to be paid at the Virginia Beach Public Works Department, at 18th and Artic Avenue. Then the homeowner had to take the fee receipt to Norfolk City Water Department, and pay for a meter ($70.00 to $125.00) and water deposit ($10.00). The City of Norfolk would then install the meter. The homeowner would then

THE SIXTIES

have a plumber connect the water from the meter to the house. Water at that time cost 57 cents for 750 gallons. See further information about city water in the paragraph on the Lake Gaston Pipeline in Chapter 6.

Virginian Pilot/Beacon Neighborhood Profile. The Thoroughgood neighborhood was profiled in the May 18, 1967 issue of the Beacon. It opened with a long lead in about the Adam Thoroughgood House, including an interview with Martha Lindemann, Adam Thoroughgood House curator, who lived across the street at 1641 Parish Road. (Note: By the way, Martha Lindemann was a member of Thoroughgood Garden Club, and served as its president from 1962-63.) The neighborhood profile said the elegant lawns and gardens of Adam Thoroughgood House set the standard for most of the yards of residents in the community. Homes in the neighborhood at that time ranged from $28,000 to $150,000. There were 650 home sites at that time, which ranged from one-half to two acres, and about 40 of the 650 lots were vacant. The article mentioned Thorogood Corporation was (at that time) headed by Mrs. William F. Fulford, formerly Hazel Collier. Her husband headed Fulford Realty and Fulford Construction Company. Also mentioned was the Hermitage House, then occupied by the skipper of the USS Forrestal, and was once the Ferrell Moore family home. The two active garden clubs (Thoroughgood and Hermitage Garden Clubs) were mentioned and one of their presidents quoted. Also quoted was Albert Harden, president of the Thoroughgood Civic League who said the Civic League was pushing to get city water and sewer service. Another objective was the establishment of a "swim and country club." Principal Daniels of Thoroughgood Elementary School was quoted as saying the students were a little above average, coming from the type of family that stressed education. The article was accompanied by several photographs – of the Thoroughgood House (with the elm trees), one of the docents at the Thoroughgood House in full period costume, Principal Daniels in front of Thoroughgood Elementary School, and the front brick gates with "Thoroughgood" in wrought iron scrollwork. This scrollwork and two post lights on the brick pillars was a project accomplished by the Thoroughgood Garden Club in 1966/67.

Thoroughgood Civic League in the News. The Virginian Pilot/Beacon wrote an article featuring the Thoroughgood Civic League (May 22, 1969). The outgoing president at the time was Brigadier General Austin Brunelli, and incoming president was Bailey Condrey. The membership was 400 as

HISTORY OF THE THOROUGHGOOD NEIGHBORHOOD

compared to the first year of the Civic League when members numbered 42. Notable achievements reported in the article included obtaining in the White Acre Farm area (i.e., near Independence Middle) zoning compatible with that in the adjoining area of Thoroughgood; helping to make city water available to all residents of Thoroughgood and Thoroughgood Estates, including obtaining agreement with the city in assuring equalization of charges when connecting to the city water system. At the time they were also working with the city in connection with a traffic feasibility study at the intersection of Independence Boulevard/Ewell Road, and the main entrance on Pleasure House Road. The Thoroughgood Civic League was responsible during this time for the installation of streetlights, drainage, and traffic signs.

Bayside Presbyterian Church Built. Bayside Presbyterian Church celebrated its 50th year in 2003, according to the Church's website. However, it did not exist at its present site all that time. According to the history section of the Bayside Presbyterian Church's website, Bayside began under the leadership and vision of the pastor of the East Ocean View Presbyterian Church, Reverend Gordon Riggan, as the Robbins Corner Chapel and was founded as an Outpost Mission of that Church in 1948. It was financed by gifts of a lot at the corner of Bradford Road and Rutherford Road and $1,000 from Mr. George W. Robbins, Jr., $500 from the parent Church, and $1,500 from the Home Mission Committee of Norfolk Presbytery. The deed was recorded in the Clerk's office of the Circuit Court of Princess Anne County on July 31, 1948. Immediately thereafter, a Building Committee was appointed and work began on the construction of a concrete block building. That building still stands today.

The Church had its groundbreaking ceremony for its current location on the corner of Ewell Road and "Bayside Road" (i.e., what Independence Boulevard used to be called) on August 18, 1963. The new building was occupied on June 24, 1964. The Church's website shows an interesting picture of its present location off of Bayside Road before the Church was built. Although the land behind the Church would eventually be Thoroughgood Estates, there were no houses as far as the eye could see at that time, and a good part of the land was barren of trees.

Bayside Presbyterian Church has been, and continues to be a vibrant part of our neighborhood. In addition to being a place of worship for many Thoroughgood residents, it hosts Thoroughgood Civic League meetings,

THE SIXTIES

provides a preschool for many Thoroughgood children, and sponsors Cub Scout Pack 364. The Church is home to Virginia Beach voting precinct (0038) for the Witchduck area. In addition, it is the meeting place for the Suburban Women's Club, garden clubs, Sons of Norway, embroidery guilds, genealogy, Stop Hunger Now and a vibrant food pantry for those in need, and language and painting classes, just to name a few. It is a beehive of activity day and night.

Outside the Neighborhood:

- **Frank W. Cox High Founded.** In 1961 when Frank W. Cox High School was founded, Thoroughgood high school students were re-zoned from Princess Anne High School to Cox. Cox started with grade eight. Originally Cox was housed where (the old) Great Neck Middle School used to reside. Cox moved to its present location of Shorehaven Drive in 1983. Thoroughgood high school students were re-zoned back to Princess Anne High School in 2001 (see Chapter 7 for more on that rezoning).
- **The Birth of a City.** As mentioned in Chapter 1, Virginia Beach was incorporated as a town in 1906, and as a city in 1952. However, the "city" in 1952 consisted of merely the two-mile resort area. It wasn't until January 1, 1963 that Princess Anne County merged with this two-mile resort area to form the City of Virginia Beach most of us are familiar with today. An article in the Beacon (October 28, 2012) discussed the process that took place in 1963 to address the hundreds of issues necessary to implement the merger on time. This began with the approval of voters in both the county and city. Overwhelming approval was provided on January 4, 1962, followed by approval of the charter by the General Assembly on February 28, 1962. That left only 10 months to make the merge a reality. Things that had to be accomplished included revising real estate taxes and upgrading street signs. The transition was reported a smooth one, due to strong political leadership and a strong sense of collaboration between county and city officials.
- **Old Donation Center Built.** According to Virginia Beach Public School website, Historical School overview, the building was originally opened in January 1965 as Old Donation Elementary. On March 17, 1998, the Virginia Beach School Board approved a

HISTORY OF THE THOROUGHGOOD NEIGHBORHOOD

redesigned gifted elementary school plan. This vote paved the way for 400 academically gifted students to attend a single-site gifted elementary school at the Old Donation Center - many came from Thoroughgood Elementary School. In addition, this new model included resource teachers to work in each elementary school to provide differentiated instruction to those gifted students who participate in the resource cluster program.

- **_Pembroke Mall_**. The book "A Collection of Newspaper Articles on the History of Princess Anne County" shows Pembroke Farm in 1961. According to Ask.com, Pembroke Mall began construction in 1965 on this farmland and opened in 1966. The original anchor stores were Sears and Miller & Rhoads. The "Back in the Day" section of the Beacon (May 19, 2013) showed a photo of Sears at Pembroke when it opened. At the time, the store was reportedly one of the most modern department stores in Virginia and one of the largest and most luxurious Sears stores in the nation. An advertisement in the Virginian Pilot (January 10, 1974) showed the other stores at Pembroke Mall at that time to include Fine's Men Shop, Hofheimer Shoes, The Hub, Kinney Shoes, Sears, Lerner Shops, People's Drug Stores, Woolworth's Dime Store, and Thom McAn Shoes. An article in the Beacon (April 4, 2011) reported that the Pembroke Theater was built in the summer of 1971. It offered a movie and cartoons for 25 cents (along with six Coke bottle caps). The theater had wide seats that rocked back and forth. An expansion of Pembroke Mall in 1981 added Rices Nachamans as the third anchor. Four years later, Hess's acquired Rices Nachamans and re-branded the stores as Hess's. Hess's sold to Profitts's in 1993, and in 1998 Profitt's sold to Dilliards. Miller & Rhoads closed its Pembroke Mall location in 1990, and was replaced by Uptons. Stein Mart was added in the mid-1990s. In 1997 Woolworth closed, in 1999 Uptons closed and in 2002 Dilliards closed, Kohls replaced Uptons in 2003. The multi-plex movie theater closed in 2011, making way for a Target store.
- **_Bayside Area Library_**. The original library building was built in 1966-67, in the location of the parking lot of the current Bayside Library. The first librarian for the Bayside Area Library was Martha

THE SIXTIES

"Marcy" Sims, who in 2012 was the Library Director for the City of Virginia Beach.
- **_Haygood Shopping Center_**. According to an article in the Virginia Beach Beacon (March 17, 1969), Mayor Frank Dusch officiated in the groundbreaking ceremonies for the Haygood Shopping Center on a 30-acre tract at Haygood Road and Independence Boulevard. Tenants contracted for the first phase of building included Rose's Department Store, A&P Grocery Store, People's Drug, and the Virginia National Bank.
- **_Newspapers_**. Most know the current newspaper is the Virginian Pilot, and the section for Virginia Beach is called the Beacon. Some long time residents may remember when there were two newspapers – the Virginian Pilot in the morning, and the Ledger Star in the evening. As noted in the book "Princess Anne County and Virginia Beach, a pictorial history," by Stephen S. Mansfield, Virginia Beach had several newspapers, including: The Princess Anne Times (began 1915); the Virginia Beach News (1925), the Princess Anne Free Press (1952 to 1962); the Virginia Beach Sun (merged with the Virginia Beach News in 1947); and finally the Virginia Beach Beacon (began March 2, 1962) – back then known as Virginia Beach Princess Anne Beacon. Also, our very own Bob Coffey (former president of Civic League) ran a newspaper called "The Northside Tattler," out of his office in Church Point Commons in/around 1996.

CHAPTER 4

The Seventies

Expansion of Thoroughgood. A small change was made to Thoroughgood in the 1970s. Section 8, Part B (May 1970, Map Book 84, page 8) created two new home sites at the south side corner of Delray Drive and Ewell Road. This included the house on the corner, and the one next to it. The land was owned/developed by Charles Bowden.

Expansion of Thoroughgood Estates. While the earlier section of Thoroughgood Estates was owned and developed by Thoroughgood Estates, Inc., new sections were owned/developed by the Herbert L. and Florence G. Kramer, as follows:

- Section 3, Part 1, Phase I (January 1973, Map Book 95, page 30) is bounded by Ewell Road, Dunstan Lane (south side), Wakefield Drive, and Thoroughgood Colony. It includes Sir Richard Road, Iredell Court, Wakefield Circle, Marshall Lane, and Marshall Court. It was noted in Civic League correspondence that somewhere along the way, this section was zoned 15,000 square feet, which probably helped make the case for rezoning the eight acres north of Dunstan Lane as 20,000 square feet.
- Section 3A (February 1974, Map Book 125, page 45) is the north side of Dunstan Lane (backs to Blackthorne) between Ewell Road and Wakefield Drive, to include Dunstan Circle. This section also includes five lots on Wakefield (backs to Dunstan Circle just prior to Blackthorne). All together there were 21 lots in this section. A review of Civic League records indicates zoning in Section 3A

HISTORY OF THE THOROUGHGOOD NEIGHBORHOOD

was challenged. In 1978 and 1979, the Civic League challenged a zoning request for approximately eight acres northeast of the intersection of Dunstan and Wakefield – to prevent it from being downzoned from R-1 (40,000) to R-3 (20,000). Based on the City of Virginia Beach's response, this area involved 21 lots on Dunstan Road between Ewell Road and Wakefield Drive, including Dunstan Circle…so the area would have actually been northwest of Dunstan Lane and Wakefield Drive. The City said originally in 1968 the lots were zoned between 20,000 and 30,000 square feet and there were 22 home sites planned. Somehow (according to the city's response dated June 29, 1978) in October of 1973, the City Council rezoned the entire parcel to R-3 (20,000 square feet). The final subdivision plat then showed 21 lots rather than the 22 lots proposed in 1968.

- Section 3B (June 1978, Map Book 133, page 21) is the area east of Wakefield Drive between Thoroughgood Colony and Dunstan/Independence Middle School. It includes Ronald Court and Sir Richard Court. This section was perhaps contested in May 1978. Mr. Kramer submitted a petition #10 to the Planning Commission to change the zoning east of Wakefield, south of Dunstan from R-3 (20,000 SF) to R-4. This would change the number of lots from 14 homes to 18 homes. The Planning Commission denied the petition and recommended the land for a public facility use. One might have thought this petition was for the land which is currently the site for Independence Middle School. However, by 1978 that school was already built. Perhaps the "public facility use" referred to the adjoining playground/balls fields of the school, or something else. At any rate, the section of the neighborhood between Independence Middle School and Thoroughgood Colony does reflect 18 houses, which was requested in this petition.

About the Kramers – all that could be found was in obituaries and Google searches. Mr. Kramer's obituary said he was born in Norfolk on December 15, 1928. He died at the age of 66 on March 4, 1995. He was past president of the Tidewater Home Builders Association and the benefactor of the Kramer Prize for Community Service at the University of Virginia Law School. He was a Board member of the Ohef Sholom Temple and the Chrysler Museum. Mrs. Kramer was born in Richmond on March 6, 1930

THE SEVENTIES

and died at the age of 63 on August 10, 1993. She was an avid golfer. They were married May 16, 1950 in Wake, North Carolina. Their three sons include Jeffrey L. Kramer, Richard G. Kramer, and Edward A. Kramer. Also, according to the 1959 Thoroughgood Civic League Directory, the Kramers lived at that time in Thoroughgood, at 2807 (or 4201) Thoroughgood Lane.

Continued development of Rudacil Land. The 1960s saw the development of the south side of Wakefield Court and adjoining corner of Wakefield Road, and Wakefield Court saw continued development in the 1970s, to include the remaining five lots on the south side of Wakefield Court – this would be 4189, 4191, 4193, 4201 and 4201 Wakefield Court. As mentioned in the previous chapter, these homes were not platted as Thoroughgood, but rather as "Subdivision of Property for Coite B. Rudacil and Clarice G. Rudacil, Bayside Borough." The date of the plat is January 1970.

Thoroughgood Colony. Although not part of the Thoroughgood Civic League, Thoroughgood Colony has always been of interest to our neighborhood. Thoroughgood Civic League noted two petitions submitted by W. W. Oliver, IV and Lillian S. Oliver to the Virginia Beach Planning Commission for a change in zoning from R-4 Residential District to R-9 Residential Townhouse District. Together the two petitions covered almost 18 acres north and south of Wakefield Drive on the east side of Independence in the Thoroughgood Estates area. The Virginian Pilot said in an article (April 9, 1975) that the petitions had been approved by the Planning Commission and would result in the building of 150 townhouses by the Sir Galahad Development Group. This action reflected a rezoning from single-family homes. Developers had previously been denied a requested zoning change to make the area into a shopping center. With the townhouse request, the developer had agreed with Thoroughgood Civic League requests to construct a five-foot buffer of foliage to separate the project from Independence Boulevard, and agreed the only access from Independence Boulevard would be via Wakefield Drive. Regardless, Thoroughgood Civic League opposed the zoning change, and petitioned the City Council to deny it. The Civic League's objection was that additional congestion from more dense housing would worsen the present already over-crowded schools and traffic. The Planning Commission said that what had been previously zoned as single family dwellings on the site was not realistic next to Independence Road which handled 30,000 vehicles daily, 5,000 above capacity. City Council voted 2 June 1975 to approve the

◄ HISTORY OF THE THOROUGHGOOD NEIGHBORHOOD

rezoning. A Virginian Pilot article (June 1975) said that a "community park" would provide the buffer on one end, and landscaping will separate the townhouses from Independence Boulevard.

Alan Lew Hoffman developed Thoroughgood Colony. Mr. Hoffman passed away on August 2, 2009 and his obituary mentioned he also developed the Norfolk landmarks including the Golden Triangle (first high rise hotel in Norfolk in 1958) and the Royal Mace Apartments, also in Norfolk.

Sewage Lines for Thoroughgood. The 1970's reflected a continuous struggle by the Thoroughgood Civic League to get sewer lines installed in the neighborhood, in order to replace aging septic tanks. This was a citywide struggle. In an article in the Virginian Pilot (April 22, 1975) discharge from septic tanks was cited as the main reason for closing the Lynnhaven River oyster beds. The city was trying more than ever to gain federal and state funds to build the Atlantic Treatment Plant to not only clean the Lynnhaven River, but also to fight pollution in other areas of the city. In the special edition of the Beacon in 1998 (to commemorate the founding of Virginia Beach), it was reported that the septic tank failure rate was more than 50% in 1973-74. It was so bad the city's health director asked the state to declare Virginia Beach's sewage problems "a severe health emergency."

Thoroughgood Civic League sent a letter to the City Manager on September 12, 1974 to go on record to express growing concern over sewage. In the letter, the President said that sewage problems in Thoroughgood were reaching near critical stages for some residents, citing that with heavy rains, some residents were plagued with raw sewage on top of the ground and restrained themselves from using laundry detergent and inviting guests over. The City Manager responded in November 20, 1974 that our situation was typical throughout the city, and the City Council had endorsed a very aggressive program for the installation of sewer lines in all the older communities, and priority had been given where areas had experienced severe health problems. However, the city had not been able to keep up with all the failing septic tanks. According to the City of Virginia Beach, the Thoroughgood Area Sanitary Sewer System first appeared in the 1972-77 Capital Improvements Program (CIP) at an estimated cost of $1.2 million. The City Manager, in a letter in 1974, said the irregularity of the land in Thoroughgood made it necessary to construct pumping stations throughout the entire area, increasing the project to $5 million. The City Manager said

THE SEVENTIES

due to bonding limitations, they were unable to plan for the Thoroughgood project until 1977. The City Manager's office wrote again in September 1976 citing the sewer installation was included in the 1977-1981 CIP. In March 1977 the Civic League sent a letter to Dr. Clarence A. Holland, Councilman to again mention there had been no contract let for the installation of sewers in Thoroughgood. In 1977 the Assistant City Manager spoke about sewers for Thoroughgood at the September general meeting of the residents. In 1978 Councilman Holland addressed the membership at a general meeting in September regarding city sewer and plans for Thoroughgood.

A letter was finally sent from the City of Virginia Beach to the Thoroughgood residents on January 19, 1979 to announce construction of sanitary sewer facilities would commence in January 1979, and be completed by September 1981. The project was broken into four contracts covering about ½ of Thoroughgood, each using different construction crews. Those small Colonial houses throughout Thoroughgood (along Dunstan Lane, Whitethorne Road, Ewell Road, etc.) are pumping stations for the sewer. Not all the pumping stations in the city are that attractive, complete with crown dental molding, and in some cases chimneys (for ventilation). We were fortunate the city blended the pumping stations in with the vibe of the neighborhood.

Continuation of the Front Entrance Controversy. As we left off with this in the previous chapter, 1969 was the scene of a contentious battle between the Thoroughgood residents and Thorogood Corporation over what to do with the front entrance. After many meetings with the Planning Commission and City Council, Thorogood Corporation prevailed and was granted permission to build 15 professional buildings and specialty shops on either side of Thoroughgood Square. We all know that did not happen.

What happened in the meantime? Well nothing for a while, at least nothing was noted in Thoroughgood Civic League files. In 1972, Dr. Baxter and Dr. Holland and three other doctors expressed an interest in using about two acres at the front gate for a Professional Building. The Civic League Board had no objections. The doctors were invited to address the membership, but never did. They instead bought land further down on Pleasure House Road. Also in 1972, the city proposed the Master Zoning Plan, and initially labeled the front entrance as R-3 (residential). This was probably a mistake, and was quickly changed to O-1 (Office). The Thoroughgood Civic

HISTORY OF THE THOROUGHGOOD NEIGHBORHOOD

League wrote a letter to the Planning Commission to change the property back to R-3, but the Planning Commission said the O-1 zoning reflected the land use proposed in the Bayside Development Plan. The O-1 zoning was meant to be a compromise between the Thoroughgood residents and the property owner. This Master Zoning Plan was still in the proposal stage, subject to approval by City Council.

During this time the Civic League had received a number of complaints from residents asking what was going to be done about maintenance to the grounds at the front entrance, which had (in one resident's words) become a "disgrace." The Thoroughgood Civic League Board noted the grass had not been cut properly during the summer of 1973 and that the area has collected a lot of trash. The Thoroughgood Civic League looked into options including asking the owners to maintain their property, or for the Civic League to pay someone to cut the grass.

In 1974/75 the maintenance was improved, and the owners further attempted to mend fences by allowing the front entrance land to be used for the annual neighborhood Christmas program in 1974.

In September, 1976 the Thoroughgood Civic League sent a letter to the owners to ask permission to maintain the grounds of the front entrance and to assure them that the Civic League would not allow anyone to infringe upon their property at the entrance as a result of caretaking the grounds, and would not allow anyone to place or remove plantings without the owners consent. After that, the Thoroughgood Civic League contracted out front entrance grounds maintenance. To help defray the costs, residents were asked to contribute $3.00 (in addition to their $5.00 annual dues) for the annual program of mowing, trimming, seeding, and fertilizing the front entrance. The voluntary contribution approach would continue for several years, until it was finally incorporated into annual dues. Hermitage and Thoroughgood Garden Clubs also contributed funds to defray the cost.

We are not finished with this saga yet.... see the next chapter for the conclusion.

Stoplight at Ewell and Independence. This idea appears to have begun in 1970 when a suggestion was made to the Thoroughgood Civic League to better manage ingress/egress at this major intersection in our growing neighborhood. Initially the project stalled while awaiting a decision by the city about ingress and egress to the proposed new school to be built "in

THE SEVENTIES

back of Bayside Presbyterian Church." This was referring to the initial proposal to place Independence Middle School at that location, rather than its present location at the east end of Dunstan Lane. According to the Traffic Engineering Division of the Virginia Beach Municipal Center, the stoplight was installed in late 1974, just in time to handle the onslaught of school buses for the new "Junior High."

Low Brick Wall Constructed at Ewell and Independence. This was a project by the Thoroughgood Garden Club in 1970/71. Mrs. M. F. McAfee was president of the Garden Club at the time. The project was done with the support of the Thoroughgood Civic League. One of the Civic League members was appointed to consult with Virginia Beach authorities to determine first steps, and to contact the property owners at Bayside Presbyterian Church to get their agreement.

Cub Scout Pack 364 chartered. According to www.pack364.org, in 1970, Thoroughgood neighborhood Cub Scout Pack 364 was chartered by Bayside Presbyterian Church. This organization of Tiger Cubs, Wolves, Bears, Junior Webelos, and Senior Webelos has long been a welcome opportunity for our young neighborhood boys to build character, train in the responsibilities of participating citizenship and develop personal fitness. The boys events included the traditional camping and hiking and earning merit badges, but also projects to feed the homeless – like "Scouting for Food." Pack 364 often conducted the flag ceremonies for Thoroughgood Elementary School PTA meetings and Civic League functions. The boys eagerly awaited annual events such as the Pinewood Derby where they would make and race their own miniature cars. Also enjoyed was the Bike Rodeo, where the boys learned about bike safety with fun competitions. Cub Scout Pack 364 leaders were often parents of the boys and residents in Thoroughgood, who led the dens while their boys were in scouts. One stalwart leader who devoted 20 years to the Boy Scouts was Chuck Gnilka. A retired Navy Commander, and himself an Eagle Scout, Chuck and his family lived on Keeling Landing Road. He was the Cubmaster for Pack 364 for many years, long after his own boys grew up and graduated from scouts. As an adult leader he received the Silver Beaver Award. Mr. Gnilka set high standards for the pack, and worked hard to make the experience fun, interesting, challenging, and educational for the boys. He died on February 6, 2008, at age 65.

Wakefield Drive entrance to the neighborhood opens. In 1972, the Civic

HISTORY OF THE THOROUGHGOOD NEIGHBORHOOD

League found that Wakefield Drive was to be cut through to Independence Boulevard and that a Junior High would be built in the area.

Independence "Junior" High opens. According to Sarah Aho (historian for Virginia Beach City Schools) the transfer of land for Independence Junior High was recorded in a Deed of Bargain and Sale from Herbert L. and Florence G. Kramer (Deed Book 1329, page 279) dated February 5, 1973. The cost of the land was $247,500, and the original building cost $401,851.92. The architect was McClurg and Wall, and the contractor was Robert R. Marquis, Inc.

According to the Virginia Beach School website, Independence Middle opened its doors to students in September 1974 as a junior high, serving students in grades 6-8. This was the year that Virginia Beach City Public Schools achieved the long-sought-after goal of removing eighth grade students from the high schools.

Independence Middle School is the voting precinct for the Thoroughgood neighborhood.

Neighborhood Watch. In general, Thoroughgood has enjoyed a relatively crime-free environment. The majority of property damage included destruction of mailboxes and "turfing" lawns (i.e., driving over the lawns with cars to make divots in the grass). Perhaps the earliest indication of Civic League action was the creation of a "Thoroughgood Watch" in 1979. First, a notice was sent to residents to discuss the idea and to explain that at least 100 volunteers would be needed to undertake the watch. The plan was further discussed in a general meeting of the membership on March 19, 1979. That must have been successful because it was then discussed in an article in the Ledger Star (March 22, 1979), where Ernestine Middleton (then Vice President of Thoroughgood Civic League) explained the watch consisted of residents patrolling the area in their cars to supplement police patrols after dark. It was stressed that this watch was not a vigilante squad. Instead, the volunteer residents' cars had CBs (or walkie-talkies) to report suspicious activity to a base station where a call would be dispatched to police.

Outside the Neighborhood:

- ***Improvement of Pleasure House Road***. In September 1978 the Thoroughgood Civic League received notice from the City of Virginia Beach for the improvement and widening of Pleasure House Road from a two to a four-lane undivided highway. Phase I covered the area from Independence Boulevard to Northampton Boulevard. The notice said that on street parking would not be permitted on this project after it is constructed. The project was estimated to cost $940,000. One benefit for this project was to provide improved access and a safe transportation pattern for Hermitage Elementary School. In the city notes, there was indication that Westminster-Canterbury used to have a sales office on Pleasure House Road.

- **_Bayville Park_**. This park, which lies between Shore Drive and First Court Road, was developed in 1978. An article in the Beacon (July 7, 1982) mentioned that a local fort there at the time, unofficially called the "Alamo," was an unintentional monument to the old Norfolk-Southern Railway electric trains that once ran adjacent to Shore Drive between Norfolk and the beachfront in the 1920s and 1930s. It was "unintentional" because the brick remains were of the railroad's old generator plant that would have been too costly to remove. It was cheaper to cover them with a layer of stucco. The stucco form got the name the "Alamo" from a group of girls and boys from a day camp who were visiting the park. They were dressed as cowboys and Indians in the camp's "costume day" program. The land was originally part of Bayville Farms, and purchased by the city of Virginia Beach in 1976.
- **_Bayside Hospital Opens_**. In January 1975, Bayside Hospital (aka, Sentara Bayside) opened in Virginia Beach.
- **_True Value Home Center_**. True Value Home Center (aka Taylor Do-It Center) opened at Haygood on January 20, 1979. The President of Thoroughgood Civic League (then John E. Reed) was sent a letter informing him of the grand opening, and inviting him to join the festivities. Attached to the invitation was a $25.00 gift certificate (still un-cashed in Civic League records). Also invited was Councilman Holland, who was asked to saw a 2x4 at the entrance (their version of ribbon cutting) to start the festivities.
- **_Zoning Changes_**. In October of 1973, the City of Virginia Beach adopted a Comprehensive Zoning Ordinance. This is when they switched to R-1 to mean a residence with a lot size of 40,000 square feet; R-2 to mean 30,000 SF; and R-3 to mean 20,000 SF. At the time Civic League records noted that Thoroughgood was rated in general

◄ HISTORY OF THE THOROUGHGOOD NEIGHBORHOOD

as R-3 west of Five Forks Road; R-2 west of Wakefield Drive, and R-1 for the remainder of Thoroughgood. The front entrance area was zoned at O-1.

- **_Virginia Beach Boulevard Widening._** On February 27, 1979, notice was provided to announce the proposed Virginia Beach Boulevard (Route 58) Highway Project. The highway-widening project would run from Newtown Road to North Great Neck Road. In 1980, the widening was curtailed due to budget concerns, but lighting for the boulevard had been funded.

CHAPTER 5

The Eighties

Expansion of Thoroughgood. In April 1983, Section 8, Part 3A was registered with the city (Map Book 168, page 5) and covered four lots starting on the north side of Wakefield Court. This would have been 4212, 4208, 4204, and 4200 Wakefield Court. This area is across from Blackthorne Court. The owner was Charles Bowden. Recall from the previous two chapters, Coite B. and Clarice G. Rudacil developed the south side of Wakefield Court.

Expansion of Thoroughgood Estates. Further development included:

- Section 3, Part 1, Phase II (June 1983, Map Book 172, page 21) was Bertrum Court, which appeared on the original plat labeled as "Parcel A" with no home site markings. The neighborhood plat for this court is listed as "Thoroughgood Estates, Thoroughgood *Hills*" and is located directly in back of Bayside Presbyterian Church. The plat recorded that Walter F. Sullivan of Roman Catholic Diocese of Richmond conveyed the property to D. W. Bell, Inc. Longtime Thoroughgood residents George Stenke and Andy Mullins were familiar with this property and said it was originally intended to be the site of a Catholic Church, prior to being purchased by Mr. Bell.
- Section 3C (May 1987, Map Book 2667, page 1) is the area on Wakefield Drive (north of Dunstan Lane) and Dunstan Lane (east of Wakefield Drive, in front of Independence Middle School). It does not include White Acres Road, but that is one of its boundaries. There were about twelve lots there: four on Wakefield Drive, one on the corner of Wakefield Drive/Dunstan Lane, and seven on Dunstan

HISTORY OF THE THOROUGHGOOD NEIGHBORHOOD

Lane. Those lots were owned/developed by Herbert L. Kramer and Florence G. Kramer.

There was a note in the Thoroughgood Civic League files that indicated perhaps Section 3C was contested in May 1978. Mr. Kramer made an application #9 to change the zoning (in what looks like this section) from R-1 (40,000 SF) to R-3 (20,000 SF) that would have increased the number of lots from 7 to 15 homes. The reason it is thought to be Section 3C is because the area was described as on the east side of Wakefield Drive, north of Dunstan Lane. The Planning Commission said the Bayside Development Plan recommended residential uses at a density of one to six dwelling units per acre for a portion of petition nine and a public facility use for the other. It also noted that a mixture of zoning districts were found in the surrounding area – R-1, R-2, R-3 and R-4 as well as R-9 townhouses – which presumably provided little support for the Thoroughgood Civic League's objection to remain R-1. What is confusing however is what eventually was built here (as noted above) were 12 homes, so perhaps the "public facility use" was discontinued.

Development of White Acre Farm. In an article in the Virginian Pilot/Beacon (May 22, 1969), the Thoroughgood Civic League identified that from 1966 to 1968, a special committee established by the Civic League Board obtained zoning for the "White Acre Farm" area compatible with the adjoining area of Thoroughgood. On September 16, 1968 the Protection of Property Investment Committee gave a report on the White Acre section at a meeting of the Civic League. It is thought the area discussed was the residential area near where Independence Middle School stands today. This was deductive reasoning since two of the streets in the area are named "White Acre" and as mentioned in Chapter 1, a farm once stood between Thoroughgood and Lynnhaven House on the Lynnhaven River. Judge Benjamin Dey White owned the property and his property was called "White Acres."

City records show "Whiteacre" Court was developed in June 1983 (Map Book 180, page 54). It is not listed in the subdivision of Thoroughgood or Thoroughgood Estates, but rather the "Subdivision of Whiteacre." However, as noted in the 1977/78 update to the Thoroughgood Civic League Constitution and By-laws, White Acre Road and Court are included in Thoroughgood's boundaries. The owners of the White Acre property were Richard and Jeffrey Kramer – as conveyed by (parents) Herbert and Florence Kramer in 1981.

THE EIGHTIES

The plat notes that all lots are a minimum 40,000 square feet – just as the 1966-68 Civic League would have wanted. The name appeared as "White Acres" Court versus "Whiteacre" Court on a re-subdivision of lots 5 and 6 in November 1996 (Map Book 192, pages 64-65).

Adam Thoroughgood. On April 27, 1985 Alice Granbery Walter gave a speech on "Our Early Settlers" at Virginia Wesleyan College. Most of her speech was about Adam Thoroughgood. Ms. Walter said Adam Thoroughgood was one of two of the most powerful men in Lower Norfolk County. (Note: The other man was Thomas Willoughby who settled in what became the City of Norfolk, Willoughby Spit.) Ms. Walter said that if any one man is to be considered as the founder of Virginia Beach it should certainly be Adam Thoroughgood for he had the foresight to start and support the development of the area until his followers took over at his death.

The conclusion of controversy at the Front Entrance. If it can be believed, the front entrance mess was still going on in the early 1980s – some 25 years after the neighborhood was first developed. Evidently the front entrance remained undeveloped since the huge controversy in 1969. In 1983, however, the Collier brothers applied to the Planning Commission for a change in zoning for 2.7 acres south of Hermitage and east of Pleasure House Road. The zoning requested was a change from B-1 (Business-Residential) to A-1 (Apartment) and they requested to build 32 units. A public hearing by the Planning Commission was to be held May 10, 1983.

The Colliers met with the Thoroughgood Civic League Board on May 3, 1983 to discuss the re-zoning request, and hoped to have the Board's approval. They explained that they planned to build townhouses on the right side of the old sales office. They planned to sell the land to a builder of quality homes, and the Colliers would try to exercise control of the design of the townhouses, but could not guarantee anything. It was mentioned during this meeting about the egrets that made their home in this area, to which the owners said to have had in the past received complaints regarding the "droppings" and odor from that area. At least one of the Board members voiced support that the Colliers could not be expected to keep their land investment in a useless state indefinitely, and some type of construction would have to be approved sooner or later. The Colliers said that if this project was successful they would, in all likelihood continue the building of additional townhomes, and would probably design some retail business for the very

HISTORY OF THE THOROUGHGOOD NEIGHBORHOOD

front, but anything they constructed there would be in good taste. The Board suggested the Colliers address the general membership since the function of the Board was only to listen.

On May 8, 1983 an article appeared in the Virginian Pilot/Beacon entitled "Residents Squawking," referring to the plan to build townhouses and, as a result would displace the egrets. The article portrayed the Thoroughgood Civic League as "very concerned" about the development's potential impact on the neighborhood, and on the egret rookery, or breeding ground. The developers were portrayed as thinking the opponents raised the egret issue as a ruse to gain support. The article said both sides were "perched" to do battle before the Planning Commission, but the Planning Commission admitted they could only consider land use implications of a rezoning application – the possible effect on wildlife was out of their jurisdiction.

The Thoroughgood Civic League called a special meeting of the membership on May 9, 1983 to discuss the new plans for the entrance. Then Thoroughgood residents were notified in a special newsletter that on May 10, 1983 the Planning Commission voted to reject the rezoning application from the Colliers. In an article in the Virginian Pilot (date unknown) entitled "Egrets win eviction reprieve," the Planning Commission in their denial called the townhouses incompatible with the neighborhood. About 100 Thoroughgood residents attended the Planning Commission meeting. The Thoroughgood newsletter warned that the Planning Commission vote was only the first of two major actions. The second would be the City Council meeting scheduled for June 6, 1983 where the rezoning would again be considered. Residents were encouraged to be present at that meeting and to contact, call or write each member of council and the city manager to state their position on the matter.

Another Civic League Board meeting was held on May 26, 1983. Mr. Sterling Webster was introduced as the builder who was interested in purchasing the 2.7 acres of land to the right of the old sales office to build townhouses. He said he planned to build townhouses like the ones built in Haygood, with a Colonial style, with a combination of brick and siding veneer. The Collier brothers were also at the meeting, and answered questions about plans for the remaining land. There was discussion about the egrets, in which the Colliers reminded the Board that the egrets used to nest at the property later occupied by Thoroughgood Elementary School and once the school was built the birds moved from there to the entrance of Thoroughgood. The Bayville area could serve as their new nesting place. The brothers also noted that they had already turned down offers to use the land for a kindergarten, or offices. They reminded the Board that their mom still lived in the neighborhood and their father developed it – and they really wanted to put up something that looked nice. The Civic League President asked the brothers if they would be willing to sell the whole entrance – they said they would entertain any offer. The price for 2.7 acres would be about $370,000.

A letter to the editor appeared in the paper (Beacon June 2/3, 1983) recalling the Colliers' past refusal to cut the grass on the vacant land until forced to do so by the city, and also recalled the Colliers' requiring the Thoroughgood Garden Club to remove trees they had planted at the entrance median strip. The writer was strongly against any further development by the Colliers. On the other hand, another letter to the editor questioned the resident's resolve to protect the egrets, since it allowed its cats and dogs to run loose in a bird sanctuary, especially when they harmed the endangered woodpeckers living there.

In the meantime, the Colliers met with the Department of Interior and the Game Warden, and as a result applied for a special permit to resolve the egret situation. On June 2, 1983 the Colliers' attorney asked the Mayor and City Council to defer the zoning review for a period of 60 days to allow a cooling off period and opportunity to meet with the Civic League and reach a realistic compromise. However, in the Virginian Pilot (June 13, 1983) it was reported that City Council refused to allow townhouses on the land near the entrance to the Thoroughgood neighborhood. The article quoted the Colliers' attorney as saying if his clients were not awarded the rezoning, they would build whatever is allowed under commercial zoning – citing examples such as dog kennels, a beauty shop, or convenience stores.

Then on June 16, 1983, members of the special Civic League committee started to discuss the idea of placing a historic park in that location, to be tied in with the Norfolk and Virginia Beach tour. The idea was to create an Elizabethan garden, continuing the theme of the Adam Thoroughgood House. They wrote to Congressman G. William Whitehurst on June 24, 1983 to ask for support. Congressman Whitehurst was a longtime supporter of Thoroughgood, and an honored guest at many of the annual potluck dinners

HISTORY OF THE THOROUGHGOOD NEIGHBORHOOD

hosted by the Civic League. Congressman Whitehurst replied that he had no jurisdiction over the issue, but would be happy to meet to discuss it. The special committee then worked with the City of Virginia Beach to look into the possibility of receiving federal funds for the acquisition of the site, but was found to be unlikely due to limited funds and many other higher priority projects for those types of funds. On July 18, 1983, the special committee met with Congressman Whitehurst, and he suggested a meeting with the Virginia Beach Mayor. The special committee met with the Mayor on July 29, 1983. He was not able to promise city funds, but promised to talk to Congressman Whitehurst about the matter. Another idea was to approach the City of Norfolk to see if they could help with the purchase as a tie in to the Adam Thoroughgood House – which they owned at the time.

On August 15, 1983, the special committee discussed the latest proposal by the Colliers – to ask for rezoning of the land from B-1 to R-5 except for the parcel fronting on Pleasure House Road, and the lot currently standing on Thoroughgood Square. This essentially meant that the land between Thoroughgood/Church Point Commons and Collier Lane – *with the exception of the center plot of land where the old sales office was located*, would be changed to residential single-family dwellings. The Colliers proposed this compromise if the Thoroughgood Civic League would not object, and if the city would not require curbs and sidewalks to be installed by the developers.

On August 17, 1983 the Colliers received a letter from the Department of Interior (DOI). The DOI said since the egrets were through nesting and had left the site (for the season), they had no jurisdiction over what they could do with their property. They agreed the birds were likely to locate to a new colony when they return next spring. Sometime after this, a newspaper article in the Virginian Pilot (date unknown, entitled "Landowner destroys egrets' rookery") reported that the Colliers cut down many trees on their land at the front entrance to make way for development.

The special committee that met with the Civic League Board thought the Colliers new proposal would be acceptable as long as the (1) homes were made of brick and were 2,000 square foot as a minimum in the colonial motif, (2) the Colliers dedicated a 10 foot buffer around the B-1 area as well as on the initial turn onto Thoroughgood Drive and Hermitage Road, to allow a brick wall or an iron fence and landscaping to be donated to the City and maintained by private sources such as the Thoroughgood Civic

THE EIGHTIES

League or Thoroughgood Garden Club, (3) leave brick columns in place at the entrance, and (4) change the B-1 zoning for the land surrounding the existing house (old sales office) to R-5 too. In further (later) review, the Civic League remained concerned about the proposed 80-foot width of the lots. In compromise, the Civic League asked to change from six to five lots on the southeast side of Hermitage Road. And the Civic League asked for the ability to approve the Declaration of Restrictions for the new home sites. The Civic League presented the formal stipulations of the Board's endorsement to the Colliers in a letter dated August 30, 1983, including the request to hold off further development until the Board got the formal approval of residents in September. In their reply on September 6, 1983, the Colliers agreed with most of the stipulations, except that the homes would be a mixture of brick, vinyl, wood or other appropriate sidings. The Colliers would apply for re-zoning on September 7, 1983. The residents in a general meeting on September 19, 1983 agreed to the Board's position. Thoroughgood resident Malcolm Higgins was retained as the attorney for the residents – although he was also a vocal advocate of the egrets. An attorney was necessary to work up the restrictions and deal with the granting of easements, among other things. It was also noted that the agreement was not with Thorogood Corporation (who became defunct in 1973), but with Danny and Richard Collier who owned this land. A Virginian Pilot newspaper article (date unknown, but entitled "Cease-fire is at hand in Thoroughgood Feud") reported the potential compromise, as it headed toward the Planning Commission's meeting scheduled for December 13, 1983.

On September 27, 1983, Mr. Higgins sent a letter to the U.S. Fish and Wildlife Service to complain about a permit application by the Colliers to clear and remove trees in the egret nesting area. As you may recall, the Department of Interior said the birds had migrated south for the winter, and the Colliers were allowed to do what they wanted with their property. In the letter Mr. Higgins acknowledges the egrets were not an endangered species, but rather a "special concern." He asked for their reconsideration of the issue.

On December 13, 1983 the Planning Commission held a hearing on the front entrance rezoning request. It showed the 20 home sites planned for the left, middle, and right side of Thoroughgood in back of Thoroughgood Square, for which zoning was requested to change to R-5. The site of the old

HISTORY OF THE THOROUGHGOOD NEIGHBORHOOD

sales office, and right and left areas of the median facing Pleasure House would remain zoned as B-1 (Business). The discussions from the Planning Commission indicate the president of the Civic League and League attorney Malcolm Higgins was there, and the president asked for a 60-day extension based on a breach of the earlier verbal agreement between the owners and the residents. The president said the owners no longer wished for participation by the Civic League in enforcing deed restrictions. Also, he said the owners backed off in their proposals to the Civic League to retain the columns at the entrance. The Planning Commission, obviously aware of the 14-year controversy with this issue and seemed to be irritated by the lack of cooperation between the two parties and inability to resolve the issue. The Planning Commission also wanted to know what the "hang up" was about the deed restrictions, which was typically the sole domain of the developers. The Thoroughgood Civic League attorney pointed out that the deed restrictions provided by the owners were totally unacceptable and contained many errors. And he explained that the Thoroughgood Civic League had been very involved in taking over deed restriction enforcement in other parts of Thoroughgood due to its observation of the lack of enforcement by the developers. The owners objected to the 60-day extension because what they were asking for fit within the Comprehensive Land Use Plan, regardless of whether the Civic League was in favor of it. Mr. Higgins wanted to ensure the rezoning plan called for 18 buildable lots (verbally agreed to by the owners) rather than the 19 asked for in the rezoning request, but the Planning Commission said that would be left to whatever is in the area of the R-5 zoning. There was a lot of discussion back and forth, but the Planning Commission boiled it down to two main things – that the owners agree to the 10-foot easement to include the brick columns, and subject to the volunteered deed restrictions. The Planning Commission voted to approve the rezoning application. On January 9, 1984, City Council also approved the rezone request, subject to the homes being 2,000 square feet, a 10-foot easement is provided, the brick walls were retained at the front entrance, and there would be a maximum of one unit per lot (total of 19 lots). This plat became Section 9 of Thoroughgood (Map Book 180, page 45).

At the January 9, 1984 TCL Board Meeting, the Thoroughgood Civic League president confirmed that he gave up on the enforcement of deed restrictions since the Planning Commission, apparently was not happy with a third party, namely the Civic League, being assigned the duty of enforcing said restrictions. At the same meeting, the president reported that recent discussions with the owners confirmed only 18, vs. 19 homes would be built. Further it was confirmed the Colliers would grant the Civic League, in perpetuity, the land at the front entrance of Thoroughgood, off Pleasure House Road, where the brick columns now stand. The Civic League's special committee, originally set up to manage the front entrance issue, was then dissolved.

Thoroughgood Square Easement. As if the 14-year controversy over the front entrance wasn't enough drama, this gift caused additional consternation. The Colliers gave the easement to the Thoroughgood Civic League for $10.00 on January 9, 1984. As mentioned in the section above, it was part of the deal to end the 14-year controversy and move forward on the development of houses in the surrounding area. The area given was 10 feet wide on either side of Thoroughgood Square to be and used to construct a fence and plant shrubbery and required pre-approval by the Colliers. This was not the median, but rather across the street on either side of the median where the brick walls and wrought iron fence stands today. The agreement stipulated that the work had to be completed by January 9, 1985.

Problems were encountered with the timeframe allowed. It took time to get a plan acceptable (and detailed enough) to obtain written approval for the plan, and it would take time to raise the necessary funding. As first steps, on January 15, 1984 at the Thoroughgood Civic League general meeting, the president moved for an increase in dues to $10.00 to cover the maintenance of the front entrance. It was seconded and unanimously approved. It was also agreed to take up to $1,000 out of the special litigation fund to allow planting to be started for the spring season, and to allow meeting the 12-month deadline to complete the front entrance.

On September 11, 1984, the Civic League sent a request to the owners to ask for a postponement of the landscaping plan until the construction traffic reduced, and also to take advantage of the natural, seasonal times to introduce any new plantings into the easement area.

Next steps were to get an estimate for the work, and obtain approval from the owners. Barnard's Cove resident Ralph Hanna of Hanna Landscape Contractor, Inc. provided an estimate of $6,600.00 on October 1, 1984. The estimate accompanied a picture of the area to show where brick walls/fence,

HISTORY OF THE THOROUGHGOOD NEIGHBORHOOD

and landscaping would be placed. The plan detailed the type of plantings. The area landscaped included the median, along with the sides/easement. The plan was submitted to the owners on October 17, 1985, and rejected on October 25, 1984. The rejection said the plan was too vague - they wanted a site plan, along with detailed construction plans having front, side, and rear elevations and a cross section of columns and fence to scale. They wanted requested plans within 30 days. Hanna Garden Center sent a letter to the Civic League on November 1, 1984, which said they believed the original drawing was sufficient, but did certify that the columns and fence would be similar to the type of construction that exists in the present construction at the entrance to Thoroughgood. They also said the new construction would occur in an area not having any existing trees or shrubs on the lawn and that damage to the area will be restored to the original condition. All this information was sent to the owners on November 9, 1984.

The owners wrote back on November 19, 1984 with nine stipulations to the current plan. The Civic League replied on November 26, 1984, questioning the owners stipulation to leave a minimum of 50-foot curve cut in the center of two parcels on Thoroughgood Square for ingress and egress. The Civic League wrote that the 50-foot cut would destroy the beauty of Thoroughgood Square. They also mentioned the timing of the project was of importance. The Civic League said that they wished to undertake the project in two phases – first the shrubbery, and second the brick columns and iron fencing, and that it was well on its way to raise the necessary funds for the columns and fencing. The owners replied on December 16, 1984 enclosing a copy of the Deed of Easement, and informed the Civic League that the owners would not allow the Civic League's planting plants, followed by columns at some later date. The owners felt (and indicated agreement by the past commitment and Board of the Civic League) that a year was ample time to complete the columns, fence, and planting.

The next reply was from the Thoroughgood Civic League to the owners on January 21, 1985 (*past the one year deadline*), delivering brick samples for the owners approval. Next in the files, was a suit brought to Circuit Court on April 15, 1985 by the Thoroughgood Civic League against the owners. The complaint read (among other things) that the defendants acted in bad faith refused to approve the landscaping plans, and delayed progress by imposing conditions and restrictions not contemplated by the grant easement which are unreasonable. The complaint requested the easement continued to be valid and the plaintiff be permitted to go forward with construction/landscaping plans.

The trial was set for October 17, 1985. On November 1, 1985, the final decree extended the deadline to April 17, 1986. The decree required the center of the easement to remain open for ingress and egress. A plaque to commemorate completion is visible on one of the brick fences (on the side of Thoroughgood Commons). It reads "Thoroughgood Civic League and Garden Club Dedicated March 22, 1986."

<u>Church Point Development and the Parish Road Tie-in Controversy</u>. According to "1607 – 2007: 400 Facts About Princess Anne County and Virginia Beach History," C. J. Burroughs founded Bayville Farms in 1919. This area was originally part of a land patent owned by Adam Thoroughgood.

One of the first inklings of a development planned for the Bayville Farms area was noted in 1972 when the Thoroughgood Civic League was reviewing the City's proposed Master Zoning Plan. It was found that the property owned by Bayville Farms, parallel to Curtiss Drive, Two Woods Road, and Thoroughgood Drive was being zoned for residential development. The area of Bayville Farms parallel from the end of Thoroughgood Drive to Five Forks Road was designated as R-1 (40,000 square feet) lots. The other piece of the farm – parallel to Curtiss Drive from Five Forks Road to the main entrance of Thoroughgood was zoned as R-3 (15,000 square feet) lots.

Then in February 1988, the Planning Commission reviewed an application by Charles F. Burroughs, Jr. for the discontinuance, closure and abandonment of a "paper street" portion of Five Forks Road beginning at the intersection of First Court and Greenwell Roads, running in a southwesterly direction to Five Forks Road in Thoroughgood. *(Recall in a previous discussion of Five Forks Road, we indicated that it used to run all the way to Chesapeake Bay).* The application said the applicant owned the property on both sides of this unimproved right-of-way and intended to develop a residential sub-division there. The Planning Commission felt that closure would result in public inconvenience, since the path was used by Thoroughgood residents to gain access to Bayville Park and Chesapeake Beach. This application was deferred indefinitely by the Planning Commission to allow time for the applicant to propose a pedestrian/bicycle easement through the right-of-way proposed for closure. The owners of Bayville Farms contacted

◄ HISTORY OF THE THOROUGHGOOD NEIGHBORHOOD

Thoroughgood Civic League about this issue, and after much discussion the Civic League agreed to the closure of the paper road. Despite being a much-used bike path by residents to get to Bayville Park, the risk of the road being paved and increasing traffic along Five Forks Road (in Thoroughgood) was too great.

In January of 1988, a representative from Goodman/Segar/Hogan and a principal in Bayville Farms asked to address the Thoroughgood Civic League at the next meeting to discuss "various issues affecting the homeowners who live adjacent to the farm." But they did not come to the meeting. Instead the Thoroughgood Civic League president reported on the meeting he had previously had with them, identifying they planned to sell approximately 200 acres near First Court and Pleasure House for residential development. Many residents who lived adjacent to the farm were concerned about development there.

In August 1988 the president of Thoroughgood Civic League announced that Richard Burroughs and Jahn Summs would be developing 40 acres of land on First Court Road with quality homes in keeping with the Thoroughgood community. There were no development plans (at that time) for the other 215 acres. The men requested an opportunity to speak at the September 1988 general meeting.

There was one concern with regards to the building of Church Point for our neighborhood. The biggest issue was the issue regarding the Parish Road tie-in. This referred to the possibility of a tie in of Parish Road in Thoroughgood to a road in Church Point. One reason given was to provide additional ingress/egress for safety/emergency vehicles for Church Point. This issue was first noted in November 1988 when Church Point developer Jahn Summs sent a letter to the Thoroughgood Civic League stating that according to city regulations, two roads were required to lead from the new Church Point neighborhood with one possibly leading into Thoroughgood. The Civic League immediately sent a letter to Mayor Oberndorf who replied that the Planning Department had submitted a revised preliminary plan and it was being reviewed. After review the decision about the tie-in would be decided. Jahn Summs planned to go to City Council to help Thoroughgood fight the tie-in. Thoroughgood residents were encouraged to write or call the Director of Planning for the city to make their views known.

THE EIGHTIES

In the January 1989 general meeting of the Thoroughgood Civic League, a surprise guest from city planning came to announce that a road from Thoroughgood into Church Point was no longer required, at present. It could become an issue again once the rest of Bayville Farms was developed. However, apparently this became an issue again in May 1989, at which time the Civic League president again wrote to the Mayor and all City Council members on July 28, 1989 to strongly oppose the tie-in. The opposition was based on Thoroughgood not being designed for arterial road traffic that would become much worse with a large neighborhood added to it. The Church Point developer also wrote the Mayor to confirm he had no desires to tie into Thoroughgood. Thoroughgood Civic League called an emergency general meeting on August 14, 1989 to discuss the situation. All residents were urged to again write the Mayor and City Council to oppose the tie-in. The issue was discussed at the City Council meeting on August 14, 1989 and all council members agreed to delete the tie-in. The Mayor wrote a letter to Thoroughgood Civic League members to advise of the decision.

As Church Point continued development, Jahn Summs offered in 1990 to again come to address a general meeting to bring the membership up to date with the development thus far and to answer specific questions or concerns. He provided a revised neighborhood plat with lot sizes that ranged from R-7.5 near Pleasure House Road to R-40 farther into the development.

In the summer of 1991, Thoroughgood Civic League again wrote the City Manager to voice concern over the beginning construction of a pathway or trail which led to Parish Road from Church Point, to provide access to the Thoroughgood House. The Civic League Board discussed this issue with residents at the general meeting on September 16, 1991. The concerns were the potential for crime in the area. Plus there was already a pathway approved and built connecting the Church Point neighborhood to Thoroughgood at Five Forks Road, and that access was sufficient to visit the Adam Thoroughgood House. The pathway issue was added to the October 23, 1991 City Council agenda. City Council agreed to the path on conditions that it be made public property, be blocked so that no motor vehicles could use it, and a sign would have to be posted forbidding the use of the walk after dark.

There was another problem in 1994 with a new home being constructed at Church Point. This home backed up to a house near Curtiss Drive. The

HISTORY OF THE THOROUGHGOOD NEIGHBORHOOD

builder put footers not in compliance with the zoning. It was brought to the attention of the Zoning Board and they denied the construction. The builder was then required to remove the footers and build within compliance. The Civic League then suggested that all residents keep an eye out for this new construction and report anything that may not have been in compliance.

Home-A-Rama was held twice at Church Point – first in 1992 and then again in 1994.

Thoroughgood Civic League Incorporates. The subject of incorporation had been under discussion on several occasions in the past, as early as 1969, but was always voted down. It was again brought before the general membership at a meeting on March 15, 1982. Thoroughgood Civic League researched and found that of the 41 Virginia Beach Civic Leagues contacted, 22 were incorporated and 19 were not. The reasons provided in favor of incorporation were that the Board officers would not be libel for suits which might be filed against the Civic League, perhaps as related to the number of community activities that the Civic League sponsored. Incorporation would also give the Civic League a corporate identity, and as a non-profit would benefit from reduced mailing rates. The formal incorporation was completed on September 21, 1982, and longtime Thoroughgood resident Richard F. Broudy, Attorney and Counselor at Law handled the paperwork for incorporation.

Bikeway Path. In October 1980, the City of Virginia Beach sent a proposed "Comprehensive Bikeway Path for Virginia Beach" to all Civic Leagues. As a result of rising fuel costs, and the growing popularity of bicycling, the path was proposed to provide and maintain a continuous, safe, accessible, practical, and pleasurable bikeway system throughout Virginia Beach. Every effort was made to link major residential areas to parks, libraries, schools, shopping areas, and places of employment. After a period of citizen review and comment, the plan was to be presented to the Planning Commission and City Council.

In the November 3, 1980 executive Board meeting, a Thoroughgood resident asked for the Civic League to provide a vote of support for his proposed bike path additions for the Bayside Borough, to include Northampton Boulevard turning north on Bayside Road, and to continue Five Forks Road through Bayville Farms "paper" road to the Lesner Bridge. The Board agreed to bring it before the residents at the November 17, 1980 general meeting.

THE EIGHTIES

The residents at the general meeting agreed, and were invited to attend the Planning Commission hearing on December 9, 1980.

Evidently some residents had second thoughts for the proposed addition through Thoroughgood. A special meeting of the Thoroughgood Civic League's Executive Board met on December 3, 1980 to hear arguments. The objection was if the bike path came through Thoroughgood it could negate current parallel efforts with the Thoroughgood Watch and Neighborhood Block Program. It was also felt that Five Forks Road was too narrow to be shared with bicycles, and opening the access on the Five Forks Road "paper street" would result in it becoming a permanent shortcut to Bayville Park. The opposition preferred the bikeway path go around Thoroughgood. The Board said it was too late to bring this before the general membership before the Planning Commission meeting scheduled for December 9, 1980. After much discussion, the Board decided to abstain from making any statement to the Planning Commission about the bike path and to bring up the issue to residents at the January 19, 1981 general meeting. In the meantime, a group of citizens went to the Planning Commission meeting and were successful in deleting the portion of the bikeway plan affecting Thoroughgood. The next step was to present the plan to the City Council on January 26, 1981.

It is unclear what happened at the City Council meeting in 1981. It appears this issue came up again in 2004, and it resulted in the City passing the Bikeways and Trails Plan for 2011. The map in this document lists Five Forks Road as part of the path, as a "signed, shared roadway." *(Note: upon investigation, no street sign is currently visible)*. Perhaps by that timeframe, the Church Point neighborhood had already been developed and there was a pedestrian/bike path established from Five Forks Road in Thoroughgood into the Church Point neighborhood.

That "Foolish" Mailbox Law. Surprisingly, the Supreme Court once deliberated on whether the Federal Government could prosecute someone for depositing unstamped mail in a neighbor's mailbox. This was reported in an article in the Virginian Pilot, January 13, 1981. The Court was reviewing a 47-year-old law that prohibited the placement in private mailboxes of "mailable matter" that had not been stamped and mailed. It was brought to the attention of the Supreme Court as related to a Westchester County Civic group that used mailboxes as the principal way to distributing its leaflets. The Postal Service had threatened prosecution. This issue was of interest

HISTORY OF THE THOROUGHGOOD NEIGHBORHOOD

to Thoroughgood Civic League, who used dues collected from residents to mail its newsletters, directories, etc. Even at the bulk rate afforded non-profit groups, it is a heavy expense.

The argument for keeping/enforcing the law was to prevent the loss of revenue for the Postal Service, and to protect against mail fraud. The U. S. District Court had ruled against the Postal Service, with the opinion that for groups such as the Westchester County Civic League, the cost of mailing its leaflets was financially prohibitive, and the alternative of leaving the leaflet under doormats was unsatisfactory. The judge also ruled the law was an unconstitutional infringement on free speech. Since the case was not brought as a class action, the ruling only applied to the one Civic League named in the case. But the Postal Service was concerned that additional lawsuits would come forward, so the Supreme Court agreed to hear the case. In the Virginian Pilot the next day (January 14, 1981), an editorial was written about "that foolish mailbox law." The editorial made the case that the mailbox was the property of the homeowner, not the Postal Service, and suggested the law should have been struck down years before.

Civic League notes didn't tell what happened to the case, but according to the website "About.com/News and Issues/U.S. Government Info," The U. S. Supreme Court in 1981 upheld the United States Postal Service regulation that banned Americans from placing anything inside a mailbox that hadn't been routed through the agency's network of processing and distribution facilities across the nation. Violations of the mailbox restriction law could be punished by a fine but not by imprisonment. The maximum fine for each offense was $5,000 for individuals and $10,000 for organizations.

Thoroughgood Directory and the Privacy Act. In reviewing Board records, 1982/83 was the beginning of the discussions about publishing the Thoroughgood Directory in compliance with the Privacy Act. The Privacy Act (U. S. Code 552a) was created in 1974. The Privacy Act, in part, says "no agency shall disclose any record which is contained in a system of records by any means of communication to any person, or to another agency, except pursuant to a written request by, or with the prior written consent of, the individual to whom the record pertains." The Board adopted the following resolution on January 3, 1982: "In compliance with the Privacy Act, all members who pay their dues by December, 1982, are hereby requested to fill out the coupon attached (to the dues request in the newsletter) if the member would like to have his/her name(s) appear in the Thoroughgood Directory. Maybe as a result of coordinating the request and processing the replies, the 1983 Directory was noticeably smaller than usual. But that also could have been attributed to the change adopted to limit the directory to only members who paid their dues by December 1, 1982.

Advertising in the Thoroughgood Membership Directory. In an effort to reduce the cost of producing and mailing the directory, the selling of ad space began during the 1981-82 Civic League year.

Low Brick Wall at Entrance of Independence and Five Forks. According to Civic League notes, the low brick wall entrance to Thoroughgood at Independence and Five Forks was constructed around 1980. The wall is located on private property. It was originally landscaped and fence installed with funds from Thoroughgood Garden Club. Years later the Thoroughgood Garden Club asked the Thoroughgood Civic League to take over the care and maintenance of the wall, but the Thoroughgood Garden Club continued to make donations for its upkeep. On April 27, 1997, a motor vehicle accident damaged this wall. Bricks were dislodged, a wing destroyed, the concrete pineapple finials were broken, as was the iron fence and "Thoroughgood" letters. The Thoroughgood Civic League, along with the homeowner and Thoroughgood Garden Club brought suit against the driver of the vehicle. The driver was ordered to pay $1,500 in damages to repair the wall, and replace the landscaping.

Civic League Contributes to Thoroughgood Elementary School. In 1981, the Civic League donated $100 toward the purchase of a new sound system for Thoroughgood Elementary School. It was reasoned that both the Civic League and PTA used the school for its meetings, and both would benefit from a new sound system. Also in 1988 the Civic League contributed $50 to landscape in front of the cafeteria.

Neighborhood Watch. While the Thoroughgood Watch program had been organized, functioning, and considered a valid deterrent to "wrongdoing," the Thoroughgood Civic League decided in 1980 to augment the Thoroughgood Watch with the Block Security program. The Block Security program was offered by the City of Virginia Beach. The city sent a representative of the Virginia Beach Police Crime Prevention Office and the Virginia Beach Crime Prevention Steering Committee to speak at the September 15, 1980 general meeting of the Civic League. The representatives explained

◄ HISTORY OF THE THOROUGHGOOD NEIGHBORHOOD

how knowing neighbors and being alert could reduce burglaries and vandalism. The program required a designated block captain to host a block security meeting for ten block watchers. There would need to be nine neighborhood coordinators to organize the block captains. Mike Conner developed the program – prior to his future role as president of the Thoroughgood Civic League. Mr. Conner enlisted the help of the boys scouts to bring engraving tools to residents who wished to "mark" their property. The Board also reviewed program proposals for a security service provided by a commercial firm. The proposal was mentioned to the residents, with no endorsement or rejection from the Board.

Note that in 1980 in conjunction with the Block Security program, Thoroughgood Civic League also participated in the Block Mother program. Volunteer homes would display a red sign in their window of a clasped hand, which marked a "safe haven" to get help if a child had been molested, or was lost, hurt, or frightened.

It is unclear how long the Neighborhood Watch program lasted, but in the January 4, 1988 Civic League Board notes, there was renewed concern about vandalism and property destruction, with an expressed interest in starting up the Neighborhood Watch program again, using existing Civic League equipment (i.e., walkie-talkies, etc.). A sign up sheet was provided at the January 18, 1988 general meeting to solicit interest and volunteers. Apparently not enough interest was voiced, since in 1990 the newsletter recommended residents report all incidents to police so that they could justify increased surveillance on our streets. Residents were also informed about the possibility of a private police group that would provide security and vacation patrol for $15 per month per home.

Outside the Neighborhood:

- ***McDonald Garden Center***. According to its website, McDonald Garden Center opened its second (of three) locations. This second garden center was located on Independence Boulevard near Thoroughgood in the fall of 1980. The website said the location was originally a horse stable and riding academy.
- ***Virginia Marine Science Museum Opens October 1983***. C. Mac Rawls, Director gave a slide presentation at general meeting of the Civic League on November 16, 1981. He would also come back to address a general meeting in 1993 to describe the planned museum

expansion which would triple the original facility to 41,500 square feet of space. Mr. Rawls offered the use of museum facilities as a Civic League meeting site.
- **_Virginia Beach Boulevard Widening_**. According to the Virginian Pilot/ Beacon (December 9, 2012), a dedication ceremony was held in 1987 for the widening of Virginia Beach Boulevard from Witchduck Road east to Rosemont Road. The service roads on that stretch were eliminated and officials said the new wider roads would be able to handle 64,000 vehicles per day in the Pembroke area and 71,000 vehicles per day east of Constitution Drive.
- **_Pembroke Pool Opens Membership to Thoroughgood Residents_**. It was announced at the May 1, 1989 Thoroughgood Civic League Board meeting that Pembroke Meadows Recreation Pool was available to Thoroughgood residents. This was an alternative for the neighborhood not getting its "Country Club" and for those without a pool for their residence. Some residents took advantage of the opportunity – Pembroke Meadows charged a one-time fee up front, and then assessed annual fees to cover the upkeep and operation of the pool.
- **_"Hampton Roads" formed_**. As reported in the Virginian Pilot (January 20, 2013), the Southside and Peninsula areas merged in 1984 to form "Hampton Roads." This move was aimed at creating a larger "top tier" market, better able to compete with other markets across the country for consideration from businesses or any other entities making business decisions. It not only opened up our area to big business opportunities, but also affected cultural decisions - from the opera to the types of shows that visit our region.

CHAPTER 6

The Nineties

Thoroughgood and Church Point Commons Development. Church Point Commons (i.e., Parcel W on the plat map) was the first to be developed at the entrance to Thoroughgood. This section was to the left of Thoroughgood Square at the neighborhood entrance, and was developed by Church Point Associates. One bone of contention with this development was when the developer attempted to gain ingress/egress to their site from Thoroughgood Drive. This request was disapproved by the Planning Commission in a letter dated February 14, 1991 on the basis that the direct mixing of residential and business traffic would be in conflict with city policy.

However, the letter from the city suggested the developer pursue the possibility of obtaining access through Thoroughgood Square (i.e., cut through the median) to allow for two-way directional traffic. The project engineer for the developer said that a cut-through to the median would also violate city policy for the same reason. The approved site plan included only one entrance – from Pleasure House Road. Later, however, Church Point Associates obtained a different consultant to pursue the option of adding ingress/egress from Thoroughgood Square. In the easement the Colliers deeded to the Civic League, there was provision that required the *center* of the 10-foot easement be left available for ingress and egress. However, no mention was made of allowing ingress/egress through the center traffic island. The Colliers could not mention that since it was owned by the City of Virginia Beach. At the time of the building of Church Point Commons, however, city authorities appeared ready to authorize a cut through into the median if the developers requested it.

HISTORY OF THE THOROUGHGOOD NEIGHBORHOOD

On October 27, 1992 many neighbors noted workers starting to break down the median area to build a cut through from the ingress/egress already begun toward the *end* of the 10-foot easement from Church Point Commons on Thoroughgood Square. The Thoroughgood Civic League talked to the workmen who confirmed they had a work order from the developer to cut through the median. The Civic League quickly contacted our past attorneys for advice, and that evening called the Mayor to ask for a meeting regarding this issue. The meeting was arranged for October 29, 1992. The City Public Works Director also attended. The Mayor put a stop order on removal of the tree in the median and promised to review the traffic flow issues. The Civic League was notified later that day that the Director of Public Works had met with the developer, and the developer agreed to replace the median to its original state. This was done by December 5, 1992. There was still a question about the placement of the ingress/egress on the easement (at end vice middle), but it was decided at the November 23rd Civic League general meeting to leave it as is.

The Civic League invited Jahn Summs (the developer for Thoroughgood Commons) to address the general membership on September 26, 1994. The Civic League requested an update pertaining to the Thoroughgood Commons project that was in process of being constructed. Thoroughgood Commons was the site located to the right of Thoroughgood Square as you turned into the neighborhood from Pleasure House Road. He was also the developer for the Church Point neighborhood, and was requested to give an update on the bed and breakfast on the former Bayville Property. In fact, the September 26, 1995 general meeting was held at the Church Point Manor House. A descendant of Adam Thoroughgood originally built the farmhouse in 1860.

Bayville Golf Course Development and Start of Ground Water Controversy. On August 11, 1992 the City of Virginia Beach provided notification of the application of Princess Anne County Golf Club for a conditional use permit for a golf course at Bayville Farms. The Planning Commission held a hearing on the subject the next day. The Virginian Pilot ran an article on August 21, 1992 to announce the project as the "largest request for development in the fragile Chesapeake Bay Watershed" and said city recommended approval, citing that the proposal had addressed the water quality issues to the greatest extent possible, and the applicant had conducted a very rigorous environmental assessment. The Chesapeake Bay Preservation

THE NINETIES

Area Board approved the plan, as reported in the Virginian Pilot/Beacon on August 27/28, 1992. On August 27, 1992 Baylake Pines Civic League opposed the permit, and expressed concerns for neighborhood wells and traffic flow to the City Council.

The project came before City Council on September 8, 1992 with the city recommending approval. On that same day, Thoroughgood Civic League wrote a letter to Mayor Oberndorf to say that it did not oppose the concept of a golf course on the Bayville Farms property providing there would be no significant impact on the groundwater resources within this general area. The letter noted that most Thoroughgood residents had wells, and that some of our residents feared the large water requirements of a nearby golf course could adversely impact existing wells throughout the entire area. The concerns were not only the displacement of groundwater levels, but also damage to neighborhood wells due to saltwater incursion.

In the meantime, Princess Anne Country Club dropped plans for the golf course in Bayville, as reported in the Virginian Pilot on September 9, 1992.

Mary Heinricht, Project Manager for Bayville Farms Corporation came to the TCL's general meeting on September 28, 1992, and presented a graphic display detailing the proposed golf course site (250 acres). Ms. Heinricht was formerly the city's bay-area planner who had done the environmental impact study related to the Chesapeake Bay watershed into which this golf course would drain. She told the membership that the owners of the property were in the process of obtaining the necessary permits to construct the course and were seeking a developer. The architect designed the course under USGA guidelines and specifications (40,000 rounds per year vs. 65,000). There was a small clubhouse, pro shop and restaurant planned – but not a full service country club.

Ms. Heinricht advised that integrated pest management for chemicals was planned. It would take two growing seasons before the course could be played. During this time, twice the amount of water would be needed. A permit from the State Water Control Board would be obtained. The course was designed with four lakes holding 200 million gallons of water. It was planned for the lakes to be lined with clay and used as reservoirs for irrigation. It was projected to use one million gallons per week when there was no rain. The well on the property was (at the time) allowed to withdraw 86,000 gallons per day. It was anticipated that would be the use – but the

◄ **HISTORY OF THE THOROUGHGOOD NEIGHBORHOOD**

Golf Course would apply for a permit to use 200,000 gallons per day in case of drought. They would probably use the existing well and drill an additional two wells.

The Virginian Pilot (January 24, 1994) reported the two-year effort to build Bayville Golf Club was moving several steps closer to "tee off." It would soon begin recruiting founding members to get the facility off the ground. Concerned with the potential impact to neighborhood wells, the Thoroughgood Civic League established a well sub-group of the Civic League Board to stay on top of the situation. The subgroup would collect information on wells in Thoroughgood, assessing the impact of water drawn by the golf course, and meeting with the Virginia Department of Environmental Quality to review consumption and discuss compliance.

On May 31, 1994, the president of the Civic League wrote the Department of Environmental Quality, Water Division in Richmond to ask about the authorization request to drill three wells to serve the Bayville Golf Course. The League voiced concern about the potential impact to neighborhood wells, and requested if such a permit was granted, to keep Thoroughgood Civic League appraised monthly as to the amount of withdrawal for a period of one year from initiation. The State replied on June 8, 1994 and agreed to the request, along with modifying the permit to the requirement to report within 72 hours for any month in which the withdrawal exceeds the permitted amount. There was further exchange of letters between the TCL president and the State obtaining answers to questions residents posed about the wells. The membership was requested in the September 1994 newsletter to monitor their wells and report problems. Also the Civic League arranged for Ms. Heinricht to return to address the September 26, 1994 general meeting.

In a special Civic League newsletter dated August 21, 1995, residents were informed that on June 20, 1994, the Bayville Golf Course was granted a permit to withdraw up to 16.1 millions of gallons per year from three wells located on Bayville Farms for the purpose of irrigating and construction of the new Bayville Golf Course. The permit provided the maximum withdrawal of ground water in any one month could not exceed 3.1 million gallons. The pumped withdrawal of ground water from the Upper Yorktown Aquifer would supplement water collected in onsite lakes or ponds from storm runoff and recharge from the groundwater table. *(Note: According to the booklet "Ground Water Resources in Hampton Roads, an aquifer is an underground geologic formation which holds and transmits usable quantities of water to wells or springs.)* The newsletter further informed that pumping of groundwater from the Yorktown Aquifer on the Bayville Golf Club might have commenced in June 1995. The use of sprinkler systems for course irrigation was observed in July 1995. The extreme hot weather of July 1995 may have required the use of a considerable quantity of water to irrigate the new sod and plantings. The source of irrigation water was not known with precision, and could have come from water sources collected by lakes or from pumped ground water. In any event, at least two private wells in Thoroughgood had a severe reduction in output since June 1, 1995. The newsletter asked for information of other resident wells that may have been likewise impacted. That newsletter generated information on 33 wells with comments ranging from "No problem" to "It quit!" Some concentration of deep well problems occurred on or near Westwell Lane, where three wells were reported to have quit and three more as having problems.

The story was concluded in the November-December 1995 newsletter. Residents were informed that new ten-year drawdown maps for the Upper Yorktown Aquifer (wells between 60 and 100 feet deep) were the only ones projecting a -1 foot drawdown in Thoroughgood. No impact on Thoroughgood wells was anticipated or projected for those less than 45 or over 100 feet deep. If water withdrawal was responsible for well problems in Thoroughgood, the new drawdown maps should occur with wells in the Upper Yorktown Aquifer on Thoroughgood Drive between Two Woods and Parish Roads. Only one owner reported a problem well possibly in the Upper Aquifer close to this area. What happened? Increased well water demands coupled with a dry summer probably lowered water levels in the aquifers to the point that many single suction pipe pumps would either no longer lift or provide the volume of water desired at the lift heights encountered. All but two of the problem wells listed used such single suction pipe pumps.

In 1996, Thoroughgood resident Ed Belton was recognized by the Virginia Beach Council of Civic Organizations (VBCCO), as being named by the Thoroughgood Civic League for outstanding contributions to Thoroughgood Civic League and neighborhood for his perseverance, countless hours of labor, and other personal sacrifices related to the Bayville Golf Club Ground Water Withdrawal Study. He was also cited for monitoring the storm drainage problems in Thoroughgood in order to avoid flooding in the

HISTORY OF THE THOROUGHGOOD NEIGHBORHOOD

neighborhood after heavy rains. Ed was honored in a VBCCO banquet on December 11, 1996.

Drainage becomes an issue. One issue that was grappled with in the 1990s was drainage, which came to a head during the severe rainstorms that struck areas of the southern U.S. in 1996. This was a particularly challenging problem in the older section of Thoroughgood where there were no curbs or gutters. The drainage ditch between Thoroughgood and Church Point running the length of Maycraft Road to Pleasure House Road had been blocked by years of brush and debris that collected there. Also culverts under driveways had sod build up. Some driveway ditches had been blocked on purpose in order to make mowing easier. Flooding was especially significant at the intersections of Thoroughgood Drive/Whitethorne Road, Wakefield Drive/Westwell Lane, and Wakefield Drive at the "s" curve; Thoroughgood Drive/Maycraft Road, Maycraft Road/Bradston Road, Curtiss Drive/Westerfield Road, Wakefield Drive/Whitethorne Road, and Thoroughgood Drive/Allerson Lane.

The Thoroughgood Civic League got the city to clean the ditch between Thoroughgood and Church Point, and to clean culverts under driveways in the neighborhoods. One startled homeowner called the Civic League concerned about "holes" left by the city in her driveway. The "holes" were the culverts – that were always supposed to be open to allow drainage to flow to prevent flooding.

Bird Sanctuary. Many recall bird sanctuary signs at the entrances to Thoroughgood, no doubt related to all the beautiful trees in the neighborhood. The signs were comforting and a source of pride – being a safe haven to nature as well as people. Longtime resident Joyce Barry and another resident were responsible for the bird sanctuary signs from the city. She said they were up for years at the entrance, and the signs warned there was a $100.00 fine for the shooting of wildlife in the sanctuary. The signs are no longer posted. According to League notes in 1996, a member of the local Audubon Society said according to the City Manager, the entire City of Virginia Beach was declared to be a bird sanctuary several years before, and at that time all neighborhood bird sanctuary signs removed, and the practice of placing the signs in individual neighborhoods was discontinued.

Last Dance. One of the mainstays of the events for the Thoroughgood Civic League was the annual dinner dance for the membership in May. This was a formal affair to mark the end of one Board and the installation

THE NINETIES

of officers for the new Board. In the early years, the Thoroughgood Civic League furnished the liquor for the event. They purchased the bottles and brought them to the dance. This was not to save money, per say, but more likely related to the liquor laws at the time. According to the history of alcohol (on the ABC Website) prior to 1968, distilled spirits were not sold in establishments. In 1968, the General Assembly passed a bill that allowed establishments to serve "liquor by the drink," eliminating the "brown bag" requirement that customers join a "private club" and bring their own bottle to a restaurant in order to enjoy a drink before a meal. The Civic League kept a strict inventory of the liquor, including the cost and the leftovers.

Records were not available for every year, but a review of records we have indicate the following years had dances and where they were held. The location and cost was provided where known:

- 1963, Fort Story Officer's Club
- 1967, Lake Wright Motor Lodge
- 1968, Bow Creek Country Club
- 1969, White Sands Country Club, $12 per couple
- 1973, Admiralty Motor Hotel (Military Highway)
- 1975, White Heron Motel and Yacht Club
- 1976, Little Creek Officer's Club, $22 per couple
- 1977, Admiralty Motor Hotel, $22.50 per couple
- 1978, Little Creek Officer's Club, $22.00 per couple
- 1979, Little Creek Officer's Club, $12.50 per person
- 1980, Little Creek Officer's Club, which was announced as the 23rd annual dinner (which meant they started in 1957), $12.50 per person
- 1981, Little Creek Officer's Club, $12.50 per person
- 1982, Little Creek Officer's Club, $12.50 per person
- 1983, Little Creek Officer's Club

In the early 1980s, attendance to the dinner dances started to decline and it became difficult to meet minimum guest requirements of dinner sites. In 1983 it was decided that the Thoroughgood Civic League would no longer pay for the alcohol and instead switch to a pay-as-you-go bar. In 1986, the Civic League switched the dinner dance to a picnic to encourage attendance of families, but in 1988 it switched back to a dinner dance at Little Creek Officer's Club, at a cost of $25 per couple. During this time the cost for the

◄ HISTORY OF THE THOROUGHGOOD NEIGHBORHOOD

front entrance landscaping was increasing, and membership/dues payment was not always reliable. One suggestion to make end's meet was to reduce further the Civic League's financial support of the end of year dances. In the next several years the League tried a slight change of venue by hosting the dinner as a cruise on the Spirit of Norfolk. The cost of the 1990 cruise was $23.95 per person. In 1991 it was held at Tandom's Pine Tree Inn on Virginia Beach Boulevard at a cost of $16 per person, but after that year it has been a picnic.

__Thoroughgood goes on a diet.__ Another popular event staple for the Thoroughgood Civic League was a potluck dinner each January. This was in addition to the Christmas Party in December, and doubled as the January general meeting. In the dinner, residents were asked to bring their favorite dish, and the Thoroughgood Civic League provided rolls, drinks, desserts, and utensils. Sometimes there was a theme – i.e. International Dinner. Childcare was provided during the short meeting that usually followed the dinner. Often Congressman G. William Whitehurst was the special guest at these dinners. Entertainment varied - sometimes there was musical entertainment (high school madrigal singers, guitar trio, barbershop quartet, etc.), magic/ventriloquism, Pembroke Puppets, or the audience was treated to a "Washington update" from one of Virginia's elected Congressmen. The last Pot Luck Dinner held appeared to be in 1992. It is unclear why the dinners ended, but the Civic League has always wrestled with trying new events in an attempt to attract as many residents as possible. Perhaps the dinners were swapped for another event at a different time of the year.

__VIADA takes over old Thoroughgood Sales Office__. After years of neglect, the Virginia Independent Automobile Dealers Association (VIADA) took over the old sales office at the entrance of Thoroughgood (end of Thoroughgood Square). Mr. David Boling, Executive Director of VIADA attended a general meeting of the Civic League and invited residents to visit VIADA, which would officially open in October 1990.

__Natural Gas Comes to Thoroughgood__. This project began in 1991 with Virginia Natural Gas offering to bring Natural Gas to residents on Curtiss Road and Two Woods Road from the burgeoning Church Point neighborhood for residents who wanted it. VNG also said all residents would be given a survey form to establish if there was enough interest to "gas hook up" the neighborhood. The plan was that gas would come to the area starting in 1993 in two phases. Phase 1 would be near Church Point and Country Club Circle by the fall of 1993. Phase 2 included the "second" section of Thoroughgood by 1994.

City Requires Clear Bags for Grass Clippings. The Thoroughgood Civic League received notification from the City of Virginia Beach announcing that as of May 1, 1991 grass clippings, leave, etc., would now have to be placed in clear bags.

Renovation of Thoroughgood Elementary School. According to the Virginia Beach City Schools 2011-2012 Capital Improvement Program (CIP), Thoroughgood Elementary School had its gym constructed in 1990. In 1993 additional parking was added for the school. In 1994/95, Thoroughgood Elementary School was renovated to include the addition of a new library and classroom for the kindergarten grade. On January 29, 1996 the school held a building re-dedication to celebrate the additions. The formal presentation included many former staff members and student alumni, including former Principals Ralph C. Mizelle (1982-87) and Don Ploffitt (1973-75). The school held a trivia contest for the event, and made a presentation of a library gift to Carolyn Caywood, Head Librarian of the Bayside Library.

Virginia Pilot "At Home" Article on Thoroughgood. On November 14, 1998, a profile of the Thoroughgood neighborhood appeared in the Virginian Pilot. The article said an estimated 3,500 people lived in more than 1,000 homes here. It spoke of how Thoroughgood used to be farmland, and in back of one resident's house on Hermitage Road one could see remnants of a barn. Signs of a silo were in back of a neighbor's house. It further identified how Hermitage Road began as a farm lane with collards, kale, and corn raised for seed at either side. The article interviewed Clair McDermott who had lived in the neighborhood since 1962. She recalled coming to Virginia Beach as a child to a place with a jukebox called the Casino somewhere between the intersection of Pleasure House Road and Shore Drive. Early residents often shopped at Robbin's Corner Grocery. At the time of this article, home prices in Thoroughgood ranged from $180,000 to over $1 million. Homes were described as "stately" and the neighborhood as "mature" and "sought-after." M. Powell Peters, past president of the Civic League was quoted in this article recalling how he and his wife stumbled upon a house for sale on Keeling Landing Road. Since Peters was a descendant of Adam Keeling, he and his wife bought the house.

◄ HISTORY OF THE THOROUGHGOOD NEIGHBORHOOD

Neighborhood Watch. On November 25, 1991, a representative from the 3rd Police Precinct spoke to the residents at a general meeting about the advantages of Neighborhood Watch. It is assumed Neighborhood Watch was not re-started since at a March 23, 1992 general meeting representatives from the 3rd Police Precinct addressed the group again, and reminded them to report any "turfing" incidents to police. In the September 27, 1993 general meeting, residents were told that the Virginia Beach Police Department no longer did basic home patrol during vacation times, and again discussed the Neighborhood Watch program. Finally on March 2, 1994 resident Harry Dudley volunteered to re-organize the mammoth Neighborhood Watch program for Thoroughgood. Progress was noted in January 1995 when it was reported in a newsletter that the program set up was 75% complete, with four neighborhood zones (and zone captains) established and warning signs posted. Once fully established, the program would have to be certified by the city, and re-certified annually.

No Parking on Thoroughgood Square. In the 1990s, the Thoroughgood Civic League dealt regularly with service trucks parking on Thoroughgood Square, making deliveries to the restaurants and other businesses there. It was making it difficult for homeowners to come through the entrance, having to navigate the parked trucks – and it was an eyesore. The Thoroughgood Civic League wrote numerous letters to the businesses at Thoroughgood and Church Point Commons, asking them to refrain from parking and unloading on the Square, and ultimately requested "No Parking" signs be installed by the City Traffic Engineer/Public Works.

Fiery Crash in Thoroughgood. On October 12, 1997, the Virginian Pilot reported on a horrific automobile accident in our normally quiet and serene neighborhood. The article wrote that about 2 a.m., the driver of a 1996 Chevrolet Tahoe apparently lost control of the sport utility vehicle while it was heading south in the 4500 block of Thoroughgood Drive, just two blocks from his home. Alcohol and speed were reported as the main factors in the crash – the driver was traveling about 90 miles per hour when he hit a tree near Five Forks Road. The force of the impact was so severe that the vehicle was wrapped around the base of a large tree. The driver was thrown from the vehicle and killed instantly, while a passenger was pinned inside. The vehicle exploded within seconds of impact. The combined force of the wreck and the subsequent fire reduced the vehicle to a charred, twisted bulk of metal. Police initially could not identify what type of vehicle it had been.

Virginia Beach Department of Housing and Neighborhood Preservation. It is unclear when this city service was created, but they provided a presentation to Thoroughgood Civic League on September 23, 1996. Speakers from that organization provided information on the Neighborhood Institute who provided training to Civic League members. The Virginian Pilot also ran an article on this service on January 29, 1996. One part of this organization was the Neighborhood Institute whose purpose was to provide community leaders with tools and knowledge to help them more effectively develop and lead community Civic organizations. They provided classes taught by the city and Norfolk State University, twice yearly in the spring and fall. So not only did this institute provide resources to train members of the Civic League Board how to more effectively do their job, it also provided resources and points of contact to call to tackle everyday neighborhood issues. And that was one thing that was a recurring theme in the 1990s – maintaining property values as the Thoroughgood neighborhood matured. That was where the Civic League's committees for the Protection of Property Investment, and Safety, Sanitation and Welfare were vital. In the 1990s, these committees were out in force. Either committee members received complaints from residents regarding their neighbor's property neglect or the committee members viewed problems themselves in regular drive-abouts of the neighborhood. The committees were vigilant about contacting neglectful property owners to politely ask for compliance to neighborhood standards. If that didn't work, the committee would contact the city for help. Committee members took action to rid the neighborhood of junk cars, homeowners running unauthorized businesses out of their houses, street flooding/poor drainage situations, lawns with grass over a foot high, etc. It was through these everyday, tedious, vigilant and sometimes thankless efforts that maintained Thoroughgood's property values and kept the neighborhood as a highly desirable place to live.

Outside the Neighborhood:

- ***Plans for Central Business District for Virginia Beach***. Gerald Divaris, past President of the Virginia Beach Central District Association gave an informative talk at the March 25, 1991 General Meeting regarding the present and future prospect of a central business district for Virginia Beach – one area under consideration at the time was the Pembroke Area (i.e., today's Town Center).

◄ HISTORY OF THE THOROUGHGOOD NEIGHBORHOOD

- **_Gracetown Incorporates_**. Gracetown is located between Thoroughgood and Independence. It is not part of Thoroughgood, but since it is on the outskirts, it is included here for its historical interest. It is in the 1990 chapter because it incorporated in 1991, but Gracetown is much older than that. One of the first Gracetown homes was built more than 100 years ago. The community is named in honor of the wife of what had been the largest landowner in this development. In an article in the Virginian Pilot/Beacon (February 28, 1996), in the early days of the neighborhood you couldn't get a car into the community on a rainy day, since rain would turn the dirt and gravel roads into thick mud soup. In 1976 the city provided water and sewer, paved the roads, and rehabilitated housing. In 1986 there were 65 homes in Gracetown with 69% of the land undeveloped. In 1996, the number of homes doubled and only 35% remained undeveloped. Gracetown was the home of the Garretts. Georgie Garrett was the longtime maid for the Mullens on Hermitage Point. Hermitage Point resident Andy Mullen remembers when Georgie Garrett took it upon herself to move into their home for a week after the death of his father – she took care of all the domestic needs of the household while the family was in mourning. Mr. Mullen said Georgie Garrett was also maid for the Colliers, and likely several other homes in Thoroughgood. The Garretts owned several acres in Gracetown, given to them in appreciation for their long service to the owners of nearby Shelton Farms. The Garretts held on to that land, despite an offer from the Exxon Corporation to purchase the piece fronting Independence Boulevard for $80,000 and build a gas station. The Garretts were able to pass down the property to their children. Their families may still live there today.
- **_Bayside Recreation Center Opens_**. Bayside Recreation Center opened on First Court Road on April 23, 1992. It just had its 20th anniversary April 23, 2012. The Director of the Recreation Center came to a General Meeting of the Thoroughgood Civic League in 1991 to inform residents about the opening and the various services the Center would provide.
- **_Bayside Post Office_**. In 1993, Bayside Post Office moved from its location on Pleasure House Road to its present location on

Thoroughgood Road. The cost to mail a letter then was 29 cents.
- **_Lake Gaston Pipeline_**. According to the Vbgov.com website, after many years of evaluation, Virginia Beach decided to build a pipeline to an existing system of hydroelectric and flood control impoundments on the Roanoke River, which straddles the North Carolina and Virginia border. The project is capable to transfer 60 millions gallons per day of water from Lake Gaston to existing reservoirs in southeast Virginia. Chesapeake is a partner in the project and receives 10 million gallons per day to augment its supply. Lake Gaston is an artificial lake, resulting from a hydropower dam on the Roanoke River. The dam was built in 1963 by Virginia Electric and Power Company (VEPCO, now Dominion Virginia Power), and was located just south of the Virginia/North Carolina border. An article in the Virginian Pilot (November 5, 2007) reported that the pipeline went into business in 1997, but the project had its beginnings in 1982. The story goes that Virginia Beach was embroiled in a nasty water war with Norfolk, so Virginia Beach decided to find its own water by building a pipeline to Lake Gaston. North Carolina didn't like it, and the two entities battled in court over the next 15 years. Virginia Beach finally prevailed and built its water supply at a cost of $150 million. In 1993, Tom Leahy, Virginia Beach's Public Utilities Director gave an update on the project (and the many hurdles encountered) to the March 1993 general meeting of the Civic League. Mayor Oberndorf also briefed the status of the Lake Gaston project when she addressed the Civic League general meeting in January 1994.

CHAPTER 7

2000 to 2013

<u>Adam Thoroughgood House</u>. This decade saw a number of things occur that affected our neighborhood's namesake home.

- <u>*City of Virginia Beach Acquires Adam Thoroughgood House in 2003*</u>. An editorial in the Virginian Pilot (April 18, 2003) recounted that Henry Clay Hofheimer entrusted the care of the house in the 1950s to Norfolk because Princess Anne County, the precursor to modern Virginia Beach was so rural it lacked an institution equal to the task of managing the property. He persuaded the Chrysler Museum to manage the Adam Thoroughgood House. But, it never made sense for Norfolk taxpayers to finance a historic house in Virginia Beach, nor the Chrysler Museum to manage one 17 miles away. Yet for 40 years, Norfolk and the Chrysler Museum were good stewards of this house. When the Chrysler Museum cut back visiting hours due to financial pressures in 1998, Virginia Beach offered to run the house full-time. But then expenses continued to rise, and the house was in significant need of major repairs. Norfolk was reluctant to part with the property, so Virginia Beach threatened to phase out annual operating funds, which would have resulted in the closure of the house. Virginia Beach struck a deal with Norfolk to convey title to the home and surrounding buildings, along with 4.23 acres of land. In addition the deed would gift most of the collection of furnishings and antique objects displayed in the house. In exchange, Virginia Beach would provide a $250,000 donation to the Chrysler Museum – which was the value of the decorative arts collection that came with the house. The property formally changed hands in a joint ceremony on October 1, 2003, according to an article in the Beacon (October 9, 2003) as well as an article in Norfolk's Compass (October 16, 2003). In 2006 according to an article in the Virginian Pilot (September 13, 2006), the City Council voted to create a non-profit foundation that would oversee and raise money for all its historic properties, including the Adam Thoroughgood House, although to this day the foundation has never stood up. *As a postscript, an article in the Virginian Pilot (July 29, 2003) said that the deal on the Adam Thoroughgood House between Virginia Beach and Norfolk signaled a thaw between these two old rivals – which could set the stage for improved future regional development cooperation.*

- **_A Visit to Grimston, England_**. In 2004 the Dean of Lincoln Cathedral invited those interested to visit Grimston, England the birthplace of Adam Thoroughgood. A committee was established to coordinate events and correspondence. Taking him up on his offer, former Thoroughgood Civic League Historian, Laura Bruno, husband Marc, and fellow Thoroughgood residents, Kim and Joe Bovee made the trip in October 2004. The Brunos/Bovees were the guests of William Howard, Rector of St. Botolph's Church where Adam was baptized, and where Adam's father and brother were rectors. Among many planned events, the Brunos/Bovees toured the old rectory, saw a stone on the floor of the church where one of Adam's relatives was buried, and saw the entry in the church registry of the birth of Adam. The church would be loaning the registry and silver chalice for the celebration of Jamestown's 400th anniversary. They also toured the surrounding village of Grimston, which today is a small village of about 2,000 people in the area of England called "Norfolk." The "debrief" of the trip was to be the subject of the next Civic League meeting. The Brunos/Bovees presented Reverend Howard with the book "The Beach" to thank their host. Reverend Howard was invited to visit Virginia Beach by the president of the Thoroughgood Civic League, Tom Forrest.

- **_Popular Adam Thoroughgood House Program Featured_**. In the July 17, 2004 issue of Town & Country, a feature was written on the popular Mid-Summer Night Program that had been put on by the Adam Thoroughgood House for the last decade. The title of the article was "Some Enchanted Evening" and showed a picture of Starr Plimpton, museum educator for the Adam Thoroughgood House dressed in a period costume holding a "beastie" that was used in the 17th century to ward off evil spirits. The Mid-Summer Night Program was a traditional English celebration of the longest day of the year that was an opportunity to observe omens to foretell the future. It was hugely popular, drawing large crowds of people who feasted on Cuckoo's-foot ale and destiny cakes. There was Maypole dancing, an abundance of live fairies, fortune telling by Magna the Mysterious, and a candlelight tour of the house.

- ***Deal Brokered to Expand Property.*** According to an article in the Virginian Pilot/Beacon (February 26, 2006, "History Has a Lot Going for It"), a deal was to be brokered for the City of Virginia Beach to buy 2.2 acres of land to the right and back of Adam Thoroughgood House. The land (at the time) was a privately owned, bamboo filled waterfront lot. Gladys S. Pearson owned the property when the neighborhood was first developed. Richard Parise purchased it in 1992. The city was interested in the property due to the prospect of finding artifacts and the purchase would prevent residential encroachment near the landmark. The Thoroughgood Civic League voted in November 2006 to pass a resolution to encourage the city to buy the property. Bob Coffey, prior Thoroughgood Civic League President, with the help of Vice Mayor Louis Jones, coordinated the purchase between the landowner and the city.

- ***Friends of Adam Thoroughgood House Formed***. On January 28, 2007 Friends of Adam Thoroughgood House was chartered. Its purpose was to bring together volunteers interested in supporting, and helping this landmark. In 2008, this organization was incorporated. Jorja Jean (Art Specialist at Thoroughgood Elementary School) was the president in 2008. She was instrumental in 2003 in helping decision makers appreciate the structure's historic and cultural significance. As a postscript, this group no longer exists – it has since been combined as a friends group for all three major Virginia Beach historic houses.

HISTORY OF THE THOROUGHGOOD NEIGHBORHOOD

- **_Jamestown's 400th Anniversary (1607 to 2007)_**. In March/April of 2007, Virginia Beach celebrated the 400th anniversary of the arrival of the first permanent English settlers to the new world. The showpiece for the event was one of four remaining copies of the Magna Carta in existence. Virginia Beach would display it at the Contemporary Art Center. The Virginian Pilot (date unknown) reported the Magna Carta was one of the most important documents in Western civilization and the cornerstone of democracy. It would be loaned from the Lincoln Cathedral, where it was housed. Also planned was a visit by the Queen and Prince Philip of England to participate in the 400th anniversary of the first settlement in Jamestown.
- **_A Visit from Grimston, England_**. Related to the 400th Anniversary, the Virginian Pilot/Beacon (April 8, 2007) reported that the Reverend William Howard of Grimston, England visited Virginia Beach in March 2007, and brought with him the 1604 baptismal register of Adam Thoroughgood, along with a 1580 silver chalice. He was sponsored by the Virginia Beach Department of Museums. Bob Coffey (past president of Thoroughgood Civic League) hosted a welcome dinner for Reverend Howard at Cavalier Country Club. Jorja Jean (president of Friends of Adam Thoroughgood House) hosted a reception for the Reverend at Thoroughgood Elementary School. Museum educator Starr Plimpton gave Reverend Howard a private tour of the Adam Thoroughgood House. The Reverend was a guest of Virginia Beach to attend a black tie preview dinner, along with the ribbon cutting ceremony for the Magna Carta Exhibit – both at the Contemporary Art Center.
- **_Age of Adam Thoroughgood House Revised_**. An article in the Virginian Pilot (July 5, 2007) recounted how originally the Thoroughgood House dated back to 1636. In fact the street address for the house is 1636 Parish Road, in honor of that date. It was originally thought to be the oldest English brick house in America. In the 1980s, however experts decided the Adam Thoroughgood House was built about 50 years later, around 1680. Then in 2006 experts finished a study that further revised the date to around 1719 or 1720. They based their analysis on an archaeological dig, a wood analysis and an architectural evaluation. According to Virginia

2000 to 2013

Beach's Museum website the house was likely built, not by Adam Thoroughgood, but rather his great grandson, Argall Thorowgood (sic) and is wife Susannah. It is believed Argall's son John added the extensive wainscoting and paneling, and created the dramatic turned staircase. Not everyone agreed, including W. Paul Treanor, a tenth generation descendant of Adam and Sarah Thoroughgood, and the author of "The Thoroughgood House, Virginia Beach, Virginia." His dispute was the subject of an article in the Virginian Pilot (July 5, 2007) entitled "For one man, house's age is much more than just a number."

- **_English Elm Trees_**. The March/April 2011 Thoroughgood newsletter reported that the City Arborist evaluated two large elm trees that stood near the front of the Adam Thoroughgood House and together with two independent certified arborists decided the trees were at a high/critical risk for failure. One of the trees had concrete filling in the main stem and both trees had cables installed to stabilize the limbs. Due to the proximity of pedestrian and vehicular traffic it was considered to be a safety issue and therefore the city decided to cut them down.

- **_House Restoration._** According to an article written by Mark A. Reed, Historic Resources Coordinator for the City of Virginia Beach, renovation of the house was necessary to repair moisture damage, to better seal the building against moisture, and to upgrade electrical and fire detection systems to modern standards. The final approved budget for the renovation was $475,000. It was in the planning stages since the City of Virginia Beach acquired the Adam Thoroughgood House from the City of Norfolk in 2003. Work began September 2009. The grand re-opening would occur on May 1, 2011.

- **_Grand Re-Opening_**. The Virginian Pilot reported (April 28, 2011) on the May Day celebration planned to welcome the return of spring, and the return of the Adam Thoroughgood House that had been previously closed for restoration. Starr Plimpton, educator for the historic house said the May Day event was planned to re-create several May Day celebrations that had been held there in the past – in 1926, 1928, and 1930. There would be a crowning of the

⊰ HISTORY OF THE THOROUGHGOOD NEIGHBORHOOD

May Queen, parade, choir singing Old English songs, and dancing around the Maypole. There would also be knights jousting on horseback and competing in field games like archery.

- **_Restoration Controversy_**. In an article in the Hampton Roads section of the Virginian Pilot ("Praise, scorn for Thoroughgood House Renovation," July 17, 2011), the neighborhood, and Friends of Adam Thoroughgood House (among other local historians and philanthropists) were greatly upset with the renovation results. Richard Stuart (past Thoroughgood Civic League president) was quoted as saying that after touring the house "you don't walk away feeling like you got a history lesson or what life was like in early Colonial America." Bob Coffey (past Thoroughgood Civic League president) was also concerned that the house was void of a lot of previous artifacts and furniture. Many artifacts purchased by Henry Clay Hofheimer specifically for the house were removed altogether or stored in the second floor which post-renovation was no longer accessible to the public. In place of the artifacts were storyboard panels. Jorja Jean (founding president of the Friends of Adam Thoroughgood House and art specialist at Thoroughgood Elementary School) said several projects were not completed, including special display lighting and installation of a new heating and air-conditioning system. Jorja Jean wrote an article for the Virginian Pilot ("A Thoroughgood House chairy tale," July 3, 2011) that called specific attention to the missing furniture and artifacts. Mark Reed, the city's Historic Resources Coordinator (and longtime supporter of Thoroughgood Civic League events) said there were not sufficient funds to make the structural repairs or purchase a heating and cooling system, repair the stairway, or repair the second level flooring. Without proper climate control it was not advisable to return the period furniture. Even if moisture levels were controlled, the city desired to use furniture and other artifacts that better reflected the house's revised 18th century history. The general dissatisfaction with the renovated state of the house led to a series of (sometimes angry) meetings between the city and interested citizens. In one meeting, participants were given a tee shirt to wear which had printed the words "Save the Hofheimer Collection." It had a picture of two men standing in front of the

2000 to 2013

Adam Thoroughgood House – presumed to be the Dedication of the Adam Thoroughgood House Foundation back in 1957. One of the men was Henry Clay Hofheimer II, and the other was Robert Howland, President of the National Trust. Soon after that dust-up, the City of Virginia Beach restored some of the original furniture to the house, and moved the storyboards to the gift shop.

- **_Starr Plimpton_** – Starr Plimpton ended a 20-year association with the Adam Thoroughgood House. She started as a volunteer and eventually became the educator for historic houses in Virginia Beach, and managed the Adam Thoroughgood House. She retired from that position in 2011. Mrs. Plimpton presided during a time when the docents wore period costumes, and took extreme pride in their interpretation. She recalled the popular Yule Log celebration and the tradition of throwing holly on the fire. If the holly caught hire, the "thrower" would get their wish. Then there were the Superstition Night Tours that actually attracted tailgate parties in the yard beforehand. Finally there was the hugely popular Mid-Summer Night Celebrations (discussed above), where one time 900 people attended.

Blackthorne Court Built. The development of what would become Blackthorne Court started in the 1980s. In 1981, Charlie Bowden proposed downzoning of the area for Blackthorne, and residents in the surrounding area of Delray Drive, Dunstan Lane, and Ewell Road had no objection. Comments at the time were that the residents did not care what was done as long as the Bowdens (who had a reputation for good work in building the houses in the surrounding area) would develop it.

In 1983, Thoroughgood Civic League received a similar, but not exact proposal for zoning change from John Anderson, real estate broker (and Delray Drive resident), on behalf of Mr. Bowden, the builder. The reduction requested a change in lot sizes to 25,000/30,000 square feet for the area. According to the proposed plat, the lots on the Delray Drive side of Blackthorne Court were zoned R-2 (30,000 SF), while the lots on the Dunstan Lane side of Blackthorne Court were zoned R-3 (20,000 SF). *It is interesting to note that at this time, Blackthorne was to be a "road" not "court," and planned to intersect with both Wakefield Drive and Ewell Road.* This time the surrounding residents were quite vocal in opposing the variance, concerned

HISTORY OF THE THOROUGHGOOD NEIGHBORHOOD

with the negative impact on surrounding home values. Mr. Anderson (again Delray Drive resident, and also part of the 1981 proposal) mentioned that the homes of Thoroughgood Estates were downzoned with no negative impact on surrounding home values. However, in support of the resident's wishes, the Thoroughgood Civic League wrote a letter to the Planning Commission to voice opposition to the variance. The Planning Commission replied that they had not received any such variance request. It is assumed the Bowdens were testing the waters with the Civic League first.

When Blackthorne Court was finally developed, it was built by Residential Concepts, who purchased the land in 2004. They built 16 homes on one-half acre lots. No lot exceeded 27,000 square feet. Exit/entrance from Blackthorne to Ewell was no longer available, and the street was named Blackthorne "Court." The property was featured in an article in "Virginia Beach Living" dated May 26, 2005, where Nancy Koch (prior President of Thoroughgood Civic League) was identified as the marketing agent.

By the way, Blackthorne Court is part of Thoroughgood, not Thoroughgood Estates. It is considered Section 8, Part 4 (Deed Book 2580, page 2157, dated May 25, 2004). And if you are wondering what happened to the original intent to open Blackthorne onto Ewell – the reason for the change is not known, but that area became Lot 1 of Section 8, Part 4 – although it fronts Ewell Road, not Blackthorne Court. An unimproved 50-foot right-of-way separates Lot 1 of Section 8, Part 4 from Thoroughgood Section 8, Part 3 – also on Ewell Road.

High School Redistricting. One of the greatest challenges to Thoroughgood this decade was the redistricting of the neighborhood's high school from Frank W. Cox to Princess Anne. Frank W. Cox had long historical ties to the community and was an academic favorite in the city. Change is especially emotional when kids don't get to go to the same school as their siblings or don't get to go to the school they are looking forward to, or expect to go to, or if parents feel their children might be subjected to an educational quality change. Families consider the school systems when buying a home, and the current residents of Thoroughgood had expected their children would go to Cox.

Redistricting of Thoroughgood students had been discussed by the city before, and had always been successfully squelched. However, in 2001, the Beach population had changed in number, age, and location, which resulted in over-crowding in some schools and under-utilization in others. The daisy chain of redistricting Beach high schools began when Landstown High School was built. The proposals and planning for redistricting were the work of the Virginia Beach School System's demographer, which in 2001 was Donald E. Greer. He had the unenviable task of moving about 2,750 students from 16 schools across Virginia Beach. All in all the Thoroughgood transfer involved the transfer of about 170 students from Cox to Princess Anne. When he told his boss he was thinking about redistricting Thoroughgood, he was told "good luck!" Thoroughgood has always had the reputation of being a formidable opponent to Beach government.

As expected, the redistricting plan drew lots of concern and criticism throughout the city, and Thoroughgood parents and students were among the most vocal. They worked tirelessly for four straight weeks to fight this proposal. In fact, Thoroughgood residents made up most of the 350 people attending the School Board public hearing on the subject, speaking not just in opposition of pure redistricting, but also because of opportunities in Cox (Japanese studies, band opportunities, crew club to name a few) were not available at Princess Anne. One of several alternatives proposed by Thoroughgood parents was to redraw the zones for Cox and nearby First Colonial, which if you review the zoning map for those schools looked like several pieces of a jigsaw puzzle. Some thought leaving these boundaries untouched was politically motivated for the mostly affluent Cox and First Colonial population. The demographer said shifting between Cox and First Colonial would result in divided neighborhoods, and besides, there were more savings possible (from reduced bus routes) by moving Thoroughgood. Another idea was to hold off making zoning changes and wait for the declining population in Virginia Beach to provide some relief, as it had already done at the elementary school level. They also pointed out the current proposal reduced racial diversity at Cox who would then have the lowest percentage of black population in the city. Thoroughgood residents went as far as seeking support from two state legislators.

In the end, however, the School Board voted unanimously to rezone the Thoroughgood neighborhood from Cox to Princess Anne. In an effort to reduce hard feelings, rising juniors and seniors would be allowed to stay at their current school provided they had their own transportation. One of the School Board members, Nancy D. Guy, said it was a difficult decision

HISTORY OF THE THOROUGHGOOD NEIGHBORHOOD

especially for her since she grew up in Thoroughgood and was a member of Bayside Presbyterian Church. But her decision was based on improving the over-crowding situation for all Beach high schools.

Ironically, Thoroughgood was initially (and briefly) zoned for Princess Anne until Cox opened in 1961.

By the way, an article appeared in the Virginian Pilot (March 8, 2005) purporting that the Beach's 2001 redistricting did not hurt home values. Thoroughgood was highlighted. Also in the September 2006 Thoroughgood newsletter, an article sang the praises of Princess Anne High School, citing it was chosen in Newsweek Magazine's "Best American High Schools." In that issue, Princess Anne was ranked #209 (Cox at #803) for its number of Advanced Placement or International Baccalaureate tests taken by all the students.

Neighborhood Watch. In the July/August 2008 newsletter, past Civic League President Clyde March explained the Neighborhood Watch program, and requested volunteers to reinstate it in Thoroughgood. In the article, Mr. March said that with the exception of Zone 4 (which had recently completed its annual update/recertification) the remaining zones were lacking support. In the March/April 2010 newsletter, a resident took over management of the program, again calling for volunteers for block captains for housing blocks within four zones in Thoroughgood. In the May/June 2010 newsletter each block was identified, requesting volunteers to be the block's captain. Volunteers were again solicited in the September/October 2010 newsletter, where it was noted that the Neighborhood Watch program for Thoroughgood was one of the largest in the city. In the March/April 2011 newsletter, the Neighborhood Watch program was still operating, and zone coordinators and block captains were identified, noting where a few vacancies still existed. In the November/December 2011 newsletter, a request was posted for a new neighborhood watch chairperson.

Thoroughgood Civic League Leaps into the Information Age. Some enterprising residents made several improvements to information flow for the residents in our neighborhood, including:

- Thoroughgood resident Ian Wright created T-News in 2007. T-News distributes news items via email. Residents are automatically entered into T-News if they provide their email address when they join the Thoroughgood Civic League. It is a way to both receive and

2000 to 2013

- send news from other residents to share information on community events, requests for babysitting, recommendations on service contractors, etc. Any Civic League member can use T-News to send their own news items.
- Again created by Ian Wright, all T-News items automatically enter the T-News Blog. The blog is the file of all previous T-News posts. As of 2012 there were over 1,500 blog posts in the T-News blog.
- Also created by Ian Wright, Thoroughgood Civic League has a Membership Services website available that residents can use to join the Civic League, pay dues via the secure PayPal system, update the membership information, find out the last time they paid their dues and if they are considered a current member. Also available at this site is an Online Directory that provides membership contact information restricted to the same rules as the printed directory.
- In 2009, Thoroughgood Civic League went online. The website was created by Thoroughgood resident Leigh Anne Pelton and designed to provide information to residents, frequently used community links, and information from previous newsletter publications. It was hoped that eventually the newsletter could be provided through the web (or via email) in order to reduce printing and mailing costs.

New Thoroughgood Civic League Events. In an effort to attract young families, the following events were created, and have proved extremely popular.

- **Patriots, Popsicles & a Picnic**. The end of the year picnic to usher in the new Thoroughgood Civic League Board evolved from a simple bike parade for a few kids to include a fire truck, clown, ice cream, prizes, and picnic, and lots of neighbors. The bikes are decorated in red, white, and blue and event held around/on the 4th of July.
- **Movies on the Lawn**. In the summer of 2009, Thoroughgood Civic League began hosting movies on the lawn of the Adam Thoroughgood House. Movies would begin at sunset, and the first movie shown was "Hotel for Dogs." Residents were asked to bring chairs, blankets, snacks, and bug spray!

Delineators on Pleasure House Road. With Hermitage Elementary, Church Point, Church Point/Thoroughgood Commons in close vicinity to

HISTORY OF THE THOROUGHGOOD NEIGHBORHOOD

one another, traffic became very congested on Pleasure House Road in front of the entrance to Thoroughgood. The school markings on the highway had become completely obliterated, and there was concern for vehicular accidents and personal injury to pedestrians. Bob Coffey, past president of the Thoroughgood Civic League initiated correspondence with the Traffic Engineer with the City of Virginia Beach to request a crosswalk on Pleasure House Road in front of the school with appropriate signage as vehicular traffic approaches the crosswalk from both sides. He also had the city install delineators (yellow and white flexible posts) in the median of Pleasure House Road at the front entrance to Thoroughgood, which limited what used to be numerous vehicular turn opportunities in this small, congested area.

"Great Flood" of 2011. The Virginian Pilot reported on September 29, 2011 that thunderstorms had prompted two tornado warnings and brought heavy rains and high winds that caused flooding and power outages. Heavy rain caused flooding throughout Hampton Roads, but the worst of it was reported in the northern part of Virginia Beach. A flash flood warning and then a flood warning were in effect for the city for most of the night. Some roads were closed and city police reported cars stuck in the floodwater.

WAVY.com reported the city received almost five inches of rain in less than an hour during the evening storm. The Aragona and Haygood areas of Virginia Beach were flooded and several roads were closed down. One of the hardest hit areas was the Chick's Beach neighborhood, off of Shore Drive. Several parts of Shore Drive were closed down, including the Lesner Bridge. Virginia Beach police say that they responded to 25 accidents between the hours of 5 p.m. and 8 p.m.

In Thoroughgood, flooding was at unprecedented levels. People were stranded – they could not get into or out of the neighborhood by car. Cars that made it into the neighborhood initially found many impassable roads, and some chose to abandon their car and walk home. Many cars parked on the street were flooded to the point of being unusable. It was recorded on YouTube ("Flash Flood in Thoroughgood" and another entitled "Happy 40th Birthday Flash Flood") by homeowners. It is wondered if we may have had a situation similar to the 1990s where flooding was made worse by blocked ditches and culverts (see previous chapter for that discussion.)

Group Home in Thoroughgood. In August 2011, The City of Virginia Beach opened a group home on Ewell Road, in the Thoroughgood neighborhood. The house was initially purchased by the state and after extensive renovation, ownership was transferred to the city. It is operated by the Supportive Living Program and reports to the Virginia Beach Department of Human Services, Developmental Services Division. This home currently has five developmentally or intellectually disabled individuals, ages 18 and older. The home is staffed twenty-four hours a day with highly qualified personnel. The idea is to provide the occupants with the opportunity to become as independent as possible and maximize their potential. Most attend the city's SkillQuest Services adult day program which, in conjunction with the group home program, assists intellectually disabled individuals in the areas of communication, socialization, academics, independent living, gross and fine motor development, behavior management, leisure skills and community exploration. Some are employed outside the home. The occupants are good citizens and due to the fact a staff person(s) is on duty provides additional eyes and ears for our neighborhood watch program.

Thoroughgood Elementary School celebrates its 50th anniversary. October 18, 2008 marked the kickoff for celebrations with a carnival and 50th birthday party held at the school. The Cox High School chorus performed, fifth-graders presented "T-Good" facts, the school community dedicated a butterfly garden, and an official ribbon cutting was held. Memorabilia was on continuous display in the school library. A fabulous "BIG 50" photo was sent out prior to the event.

The Thoroughgood newsletter (July/August 2008) announced Thoroughgood Elementary School celebrated its 50th year in 2008. Its motto for the occasion was "50 Years Strong – Good as Gold. Thoroughgood Elementary 1958-2008." The article recalled that Elvis topped the charts and Dr. Suess' Cat in the Hat was all the rage when the doors opened in 1958.

Irene Bowers, correspondent for the Virginian Pilot and fellow Thoroughgood resident, wrote an article for the school's anniversary in the Virginian Pilot (October 12, 2008). Mrs. Bowers interviewed Thoroughgood resident Amy Howard for the article. Amy is the daughter of Richard Collier and granddaughter of James Collier, developer of the Thoroughgood neighborhood. Mrs. Howard attended Thoroughgood Elementary School as a child. In the article Mrs. Howard said that her grandfather donated the land for Thoroughgood Elementary School to the city in 1956. She also noted her husband (Scott Howard) was a fourth-grade teacher who taught in her

HISTORY OF THE THOROUGHGOOD NEIGHBORHOOD

old sixth-grade classroom. Principal Cheryl Zigrang was quoted as saying the students raised money over the years to purchase artifacts for the Adam Thoroughgood House, and in 2007 they raised enough money to purchase a historic marker on Shore Drive.

Also as reported in the Virginian Pilot (September 28, 2010), a wall heater caught fire at Thoroughgood Elementary School. The fire caused some damage to a kindergarten classroom at Thoroughgood Elementary School. A passer-by saw smoke coming out of a vent at the school, Ramsey said. No one was in the building at the time. Firefighters received the call at 12:17 p.m. and had the fire under control by 12:55 p.m. The fire was accidental, and no one was injured, Ramsey said.

Bear Carving. Residents on Country Club Circle turned an eyesore into a thing of beauty. A strong summer storm in 2011 downed a large pecan tree in the backyard of Gloria Thimlar's family home. The tree was located near Thoroughgood Lane not far from the Adam Thoroughgood House. The Thimlars had the downed tree removed but daughter Claire suggested doing something with the remaining tree trunk that would leave a lasting legacy of their family for the neighborhood. So in 2012, the family hired a wood carver to carve an approximately 12-foot tall bear standing on the tree trunk base. The choice of a bear was based on the Disney movie "Brother Bear" where the bear symbolized family. The bear, carved in a full standing position, is the natural color of the tree trunk, except for the bear's claws, which were painted black. The Thimlars plan to seal the bear with a clear shellac to protect it from moisture and termite damage.

Storm Drain Marker Program. In October 2012, residents in the Thoroughgood neighborhood participated in a volunteer project offered by the City of Virginia Beach called the Storm Drain Marker Program. The objective of the project was to improve public awareness of the environmental effects of dumping in storm drains and the resulting water quality issues. The city reported that 50% of pollution in the Chesapeake Bay was due to storm water runoff. Water that runs off streets and buildings picks up litter, motor oil, excess fertilizer and other pollutants as it makes its way into natural waters. This program provided volunteers with 4-inch stainless steel markers to attach to neighborhood storm drains to alert residents into which watershed the storm drain flowed. First an inventory of storm drains was conducted – and close to 200 were found in the neighborhood. City officials provided

2000 to 2013

the watershed for each drain listed – and it was found that watersheds for Thoroughgood were not only the Lynnhaven River, but many drains emptied into Little Creek as well. Once the inventory was complete, the city provided all the necessary materials and the volunteers attached the markers.

Outside the Neighborhood:

- **Bayside Area Branch Library and 3rd Precinct Police Station.** Bayside Area Branch Library and 3rd Precinct Police Station opened new buildings at Haygood. The new library was built in 2005, and replaced the old library that stood in the area of its current parking lot, and constructed in 1966/67. An interesting event offered annually in May by the City of Virginia Beach, Department of Libraries is the Bayside History Trail. On the designated day, participants are given a passport and an opportunity to visit Bayside historical sites, for a free tour of the properties. Sometimes the properties host craft demonstrations, or enactments. Passports are stamped at each site, and participants return the passport to the Bayside Area Library on the same day to receive a commemorative pin. The historical sites include the Adam Thoroughgood House, the Lynnhaven House, Ferry Plantation House, Pembroke Manor House, Old Donation Episcopal Church, Morning Star Baptist Church, and the Chapel at Haygood United Methodist Church. This is an excellent way to learn about our interesting and history-rich borough.
- **Pleasure House Road.** As provided in Chapter 1 of this book, an article in the Virginian Pilot (July 20, 2007) said that Pleasure House Road referred to a tavern dating to the 1600s or 1700s, and not a brothel, as some may have assumed. The tavern was believed to be owned by the widow of Adam Thoroughgood, or to one of Thoroughgood's descendants. The tavern may have been located near the current road, perhaps at the old Bayville Farms, off First Court Road. That was not the first time Pleasure House Road was written about. The Virginian Pilot/Beacon also did an article "Checkered Past surrounds Pleasure House" on September 19, 1982. It was written by Mary R. Barrow, assumed to be same Mary Reid Barrow who writes today in the Beacon about nature and wildlife in the area. Ms. Reid Barrow wrote that Pleasure House referred to an inn or ordinary and its presence could be traced back as far

as the late 18th century. She said that by 1790, the tavern must have established such a fine reputation that a road known as Pleasure House Road was also located on a map of that era. Later the nearby lake was also named after that tavern. Ms. Reid Barrow said it was probably during the War of 1812 that Pleasure House gained its infamous reputation. The house was in a perfect location, overlooking the Chesapeake Bay, to serve as a lookout point for the local militia watching for British ships entering Hampton Roads. Ms. Reid Barrow said the house proved too much of a temptation for the untrained soldiers. Instead of keeping watch, they tended to partake in the spirits and card games. In the summer of 1812 the British landed a scouting party on the beach, marched in, took the guardhouse and set it (along with Pleasure House) on fire. Later a report made to the Virginia governor said that Pleasure House was a place that had not one requisite for a military location, or military security.

- **_Lynnhaven River Cleanup_**. The May/June 2008 Thoroughgood newsletter provided an update on the health of the Lynnhaven River based on the visit by Karen Forget who addressed the January 2008 general meeting of the Civic League. Ms. Forget represented Lynnhaven River Now, a grassroots organization whose goal was to clean up the river. She said that Thoroughgood residents live in the Lynnhaven River watershed. A watershed is an area of land that drains to a common point. She said that (at the time) half of the city's population lived in the watershed, and 35% of the land was a wet impervious surface – meaning it didn't absorb water, but rather, drained it off. The run-off can contain contaminates such as bacteria, toxins, dog waste, grass clippings, fertilizer, and herbicides – most of which come from homeowners. Not surprisingly, the Lynnhaven River's water quality problems grew as the city's population grew. The most alarming loss of habitat caused by the run-off was the loss of Lynnhaven oyster reefs. Since the Chesapeake Bay Preservation Act passed in 1990, the Lynnhaven River has been measurably cleaner. All storm water run-offs were required to go through pre-treatment before running into the river, but it only applied to new development. Boating regulations reduced the amount of waste and emissions from recreational boating. As a result, oyster restoration was showing improvement. Other than providing an update on the clean up efforts, Ms. Forget told the residents what they could do to help. In the January/February 2011 newsletter, an article provided an update on dredging the Lynnhaven River as applicable to Thoroughgood waterfront property owners. The article identified a Special Service District (SSD) formed by the City of Virginia Beach aimed at dredging the coves and channels of the Lynnhaven River. If 81% of the waterfront homeowners agreed, they would be assessed an additional fee on their property taxes to fund approximately 80% of the surveying, engineering, permitting, project management, and dredging of their channels. The 20% balance would be funded by the city. The dredging would improve and preserve river access and water quality. Previous Thoroughgood Civic League president Larry LaRue volunteered to maintain a spreadsheet of all the Thoroughgood waterfront property owners and to keep them informed of progress, events, and meetings. Mr. LaRue said at the time the city encouraged the effort and committed to providing a site to receive the dredge material. The Thoroughgood Civic League partnered with Church Point and formed an LLC, raising money from waterfront owners to conduct a survey of the coves and begin the permitting process. As the project progressed, the disposal site became more of an issue and the city became "less committed" to help with the project. As fuel prices spiraled up, the dredging costs rose to unaffordable levels. Property owners withdrew from the project because of cost.

- ***Post Office Contract Unit***. The January/February 2010 newsletter announced a new U.S. Post Office Contract Unit opened at Budget Travel, 1143 Independence Boulevard – next to Taylor Do-It Center.
- ***Sentara Bayside.*** Sentara Bayside Hospital moved all of its 158 in-patient beds to Sentara Princess Anne when the Princess Anne facility opened in 2011. Sentara Bayside changed its name to Sentara Independence and began offering outpatient and emergency services only.
- ***Virginia Beach's 50th Anniversary***. The City of Virginia Beach celebrated its 50th anniversary on January 1, 2013. As reported in the Beacon on January 17, 2013, the kickoff was held at the Cape

HISTORY OF THE THOROUGHGOOD NEIGHBORHOOD

Henry Lighthouse on January 19, 2013 where Mayor Will Sessoms was given the key to the lighthouse and all members of the City Council were named honorary lighthouse keepers. The city planned festivities all year long, culminating in a street festival in October on the beach.

CHAPTER 8

Who's Who

There have been some pretty influential people that have lived in Thoroughgood over the years. We have had plenty of lawyers, doctors, dentists, and certainly the military is represented here in great numbers. Some of those lawyers have provided legal advice and/or represented the Civic League in dealing with property issues over the years. This list, however, will be limited to those people having high influence in government or military, business leaders in the community….or those with an interesting story to tell.

Adam Thoroughgood. As our first and foremost Who's Who, we must start with our neighborhood's namesake, Adam Thoroughgood. As described in Paul Clancy's story in the June 24, 2012 edition of the Virginian Pilot, Adam Thoroughgood first came to America as an 18-year old indentured servant. After working off his indenture, he returned to England to recruit others to settle in America. In return, he was given 50 acres per person – a total of 5,350 for the 105 indentured servants he brought, along with himself and his wife Sarah. His acreage was located on the western shore of what was known as the Chesopean River. He renamed it the Lynnhaven River – after his home in Grimston-King's Lynn in Norfolk County, England. He was born in 1604 and died in 1640. In those short 36 years he accomplished plenty. According to "The Bayside History Trail….A View From the Water" Adam Thoroughgood was an elected member of the House of Burgesses ad the Governor's Council. He was appointed Commissioner (Justice) and later Commander (Presiding Justice) of the County. He donated land for the first church of the Lynnhaven Parish, which was built in 1639 at Church Point. He

HISTORY OF THE THOROUGHGOOD NEIGHBORHOOD

drew the boundaries for Lynnhaven Parish, which later became the boundaries of Princess Anne County and then later almost exactly the boundaries of Virginia Beach.

Grace M. Keeler - although she predates our neighborhood's development, Grace Myra Keeler is an important figure to our neighborhood's history nevertheless. Ms. Keeler was a previous owner of land in our neighborhood, and she donated some of that land to build the Skinner School. From sources at the Adam Thoroughgood House, in 1906 Grace and her brothers John D. Keeler and Rufus P. Keeler purchased 248.95 acres of land in Thoroughgood, which included the Adam Thoroughgood House (Deed Book 77, page 382). In 1922 John D. Keeler and his wife transferred their 1/3 interest to Grace Keeler (Deed Book 113, page 110). In 1930 Rufus Keeler transferred his 1/3 interest to her (Deed Book 159, page 48). In 1941 Grace Keeler sold the property to Thorowgood (sic) Manor, Inc. (Deed Book 209, page 33). In 1944 Thorowgood Manor, Inc. sold the property to Greenbrier Farms, Inc. (Deed Book 224, page 585). Greenbrier Farms, Inc. sold the property to Thorogood Corporation/James N. Collier on February 28, 1955 (Deed Book 394, page 459). Thorogood Corporation sold a portion of the property to the Adam Thoroughgood House Foundation on August 1, 1955 (Deed Book 418, page 596).

Ms. Keeler was integral to the preservation of the Adam Thoroughgood House. In 1923 she restored the house. Charles Cornelius, furniture curator for the New York City's Metropolitan Museum of Art had some uncertain role in the restoration. According to the book "Old Houses in Princess Anne County," by Sadie Scott Kellam and V. Hope Kellam, 1958 "it is due to her (Grace Keeler) that we have so splendidly preserved what must be one of the oldest brick homes in English-speaking America. Ms. Keeler has not spared money, time or personal care in her work on restoration. Also the present owner (i.e., Ms. Keeler) has been most generous in sharing her treasure with those pilgrims who come to see, and stop to marvel at so perfect a shrine." In an article in the Virginian Pilot/Beacon (May 18, 1967) Martha Lindemann (then curator of the Adam Thoroughgood House) said that Grace Keeler's restoration in 1923 probably saved the house.

In a brochure available at the Sergeant Memorial Collection inside the Pretlow Anchor Branch Library, the Thoroughgood House was advertised as open to visitors. There was no date to the brochure but was marked as Grace

Keeler as the owner. An interesting part was the directions provided for how to get to the house. If coming from Norfolk, travelers were advised to travel down "Princess Anne Road via Water Works Road; turn left on Water Works, then turn left at Robbins Store which was ¼ mile from the gate." If coming from Ocean View, travelers were instructed to "take Ocean Shore Drive, turn right at Chesapeake Beach Corner, then ½ mile to the gate."

Ms. Keeler was born September 23, 1878. She died on November 29, 1958 at age 80 in Menands, New York.

Benjamin Dey White. As mentioned in Chapter 5 (The Eighties), the area in Thoroughgood near Independence Middle School named White Acre Road/Court is on land previously owned by Judge Benjamin Dey White. The website for Old Donation Episcopal Church provides a biographical sketch of Benjamin Dey White. He was born December 10, 1868 and died April 5, 1946, and was the Senior Warden of Donation Church during its reconstruction in 1916. Judge White was celebrated as the *"first citizen of Princess Anne County."* He was an ardent preservationist of animals, books, history, and the law. Judge White presided over the Princess Anne County 28th Judicial Circuit Court for 38 years, serving as attorney and judge in the courthouse until his death in 1946. He accumulated an extensive library, the largest in Princess Anne County, which held valuable Princess Anne County deeds and records. From this wealth of information, Judge White became known as one of the best authorities on the history of Princess Anne County. Judge White contributed liberally to the Society for the Prevention of the Cruelty to Animals and had a great love of trees, wildlife, and birds. In 1924 he wrote *Gleanings in the History of Princess Anne County*. The book includes one of the most exhaustive studies of the trial of Grace Sherwood for allegedly practicing witchcraft and historic sketches that cover the history of Princess Anne County (now Virginia Beach) from 1606 to 1861. The book was re-published in 1991 on the 300th anniversary of the forming of Princess Anne County. Judge White's hand was felt, unobtrusively, behind nearly all phases of the county's progress, and he served as the mentor for another Thoroughgood resident, A. E. Ewell.

On the website for Old Donation Church (in their Old Donation History section), there is a picture of Judge White's White Acre home (taken before it was demolished in 1983). The narrative says "Judge White purchased his ancestral home White Acre, built in the 1850's on several hundred acres

HISTORY OF THE THOROUGHGOOD NEIGHBORHOOD

overlooking the southwestern branch of the Lynnhaven River at Witchduck Bay (*today's White Acres Court*), and restored it to its old-time charm. White Acre was one of the most prominent show places on the Lynnhaven River in its day and Judge White hosted annual oyster roasts for the church and neighbors until 1934 when the roast moved to the church grounds."

The Ewells. Thoroughgood address: 4124 Ewell Road.

- A. E. Ewell owned A. E. Ewell Lynnhaven Oysters. He was a member of the Virginia House of Delegates, representing Princess Anne County in 1899–1901, and then again from 1920-1923. Mr. Ewell followed those terms with four years on the County Board of Supervisors, and served on the Game and Fisheries Commission in Kempsville. For more than half a century he played a leading role in the development of Princess Anne County, and particularly in the development of Chesapeake Beach. He was a member of the original planning committee that played a large part in the construction of the first paved road from Norfolk to Virginia Beach. He was a former President of the Norfolk Truckers Exchange, and served on the School Board and Red Cross.
- Louise Hooper Ewell was a descendant of William Hooper who was one of the original signers of the Declaration of Independence. Mrs. Ewell was one of the first five graduates of Sweet Briar College, class of 1910. She organized and was the first president of the Princess Anne Woman's Club, and helped form the Princess Anne Historical Society. Mrs. Ewell was largely responsible for raising money for the people of Princess Anne County to build the Tidewater Victory Memorial Hospital. This hospital for tuberculosis patients opened in 1937 in the same building that now houses Willis Furniture.

James Nathan Collier. Mr. Collier would have made this list just by virtue of the fact that he developed this wonderful neighborhood, but like Adam Thoroughgood who also died at a young age, Mr. Collier accomplished a lot in his short 38 years. An article in the Virginian Pilot (May 17, 1957) said he was president of Thorogood Corporation (which developed Thoroughgood) and Eastern Realty Corporation (which developed part of Baylake Pines). He was part owner of Consolidated Construction Company with his brother Clyde. Mr. Collier's other business interests were Cosmo Corporation and Pioneer Holding Company. That's pretty impressive for a man who came to Norfolk after the war, and initially started a business to construct garages.

L. Charles Burlage – Thoroughgood Civic League's first president from 1957 to 1959. His obituary said that despite his elementary education stopping at the 8th grade, Mr. Burlage went on to attain five college degrees from the College of William and Mary, graduating with honors. He served in World War II and Korean War. He was the co-founder of the Virginia Beach Council of Civic Organizations (VBCCO), and on the seven-man steering committee for the merger of Virginia Beach with Princess Anne County. He served on the Board of the Virginia Beach General Hospital, wrote newspaper columns for three weekly newspapers, and appeared on the stage. He was a CPA and practiced law, and operated eight Burger Chef restaurants in Tidewater. He owned The Breakers Hotel on 25th Street, and opened the Holiday Inn on that same site. He wrote and published three books on philosophy, religion, and ethics. According to longtime resident George Stenke, Lake Charles is named after L. Charles Burlage. Thoroughgood address: 1636 Wakefield Drive.

The Middletons -

- B. R. (Beverly Randolph) Middleton was the Thoroughgood Civic League president in 1964/65. He was an electrical engineer and was the president of Middleton Construction Company. According to the Perry Library at ODU, Mr. Middleton was a member of the Virginia House of Delegates representing the City of Virginia Beach from 1968-74. As a delegate he served on the following committees: Appropriations, Education, Roads, Chesapeake Bay and its Tributaries, and Conservation and Natural Resources. The Governor appointed Mr. Middleton to the Virginia Housing Study Commission and the State Board of Housing and Development. He also served on the Chesapeake Bay Bridge Tunnel Commission and the General Advisory Council for Vocational Education in Virginia Beach Schools. He was the president of the Suburban Kiwanis Club.
- Ernestine K. Middleton was the first female president of the Thoroughgood Civic League in 1980/81, and then served again as president in 1998/99. Mrs. Middleton was the only resident inducted as an honorary lifetime member in the Thoroughgood Civic League. She was Thoroughgood Elementary School's librarian for

HISTORY OF THE THOROUGHGOOD NEIGHBORHOOD

over six years, beginning in 1962. Prior to her "retirement" after marrying B. R. Middleton in 1975, she opened Kempsville Junior High School and VOTECH near the Princess Anne Courthouse. She has been a member of the Thoroughgood Garden Club since 1976, a member of the Suburban Woman's Club, a member of the American Association of University Women, serves on the Symphony Board, and was the first president of the Virginia Symphony League. She is on the Board of the Princess Anne/Virginia Beach Historical Society. The Governor of Virginia appointed her to the State Erosion Commission, which she chaired for eight years, and City Council placed her on the Arts and Humanities Commission. She is about to end service on the Virginia Beach Public Library Board, and the Governor appointed her to serve on the Library of Virginia Board. She is an elder at Bayside Presbyterian Church.
- Barry Knight (the Middleton's son) is a Delegate to the General Assembly for the 81st District.
- Their home was at 1612 Wakefield Drive. It was a pie shaped lot on about 2.5 acres on Lake Charles. This home was the scene of many a social function. It was opened three times for the Thoroughgood Garden Tour, hosted the Holiday House, and Flower Show. Their dining room table could seat 18 comfortably. The house was built out of brick from an old church in downtown Norfolk, and the second floor of the garage reused the old gym floor from Old Dominion University. It was the same wood floor last played on by the Lady Monarchs when they won the National Championship.

Admiral John K. Beling – According to an article in the Washington Post (November 17, 2010) Admiral Beling had a naval career that spanned 32 years, but is perhaps best known and admired for his duty as Commanding Officer of the aircraft carrier USS Forrestal from May 1966 to September 1967. During combat operations to support raids on North Vietnam in July 1967, an uncontrolled fire broke out on the flight deck. The fire was due to an electrical malfunction that caused a misfire on a rocket from a taxied F-4 Phantom. *(Note: the rocket, shooting across the flight deck, struck a jet piloted by Lt. Commander John McCain, the future U.S. Senator and 2008 Republican presidential candidate.)* The rocket fire pierced the 200-pound fuel tank of McCain's plane, and fuel from his jet gushed onto the Forrestal's

WHO'S WHO

deck. Hot propellant from the errant rocket ignited the spilled fuel, causing an inferno. That fire and subsequent explosions killed 134 men and seriously injured many others. Admiral Beling's critical decisions during the disaster and calm assurance of the crew are credited with helping to bring the ship to safe harbor. Admiral Beling died on November 5, 2010. Thoroughgood address: Hermitage House from 1965-1977.

Admiral Elmo R. Zumwalt – served as Chief of Naval Operations from 1 July 1970 to 29 June 1974. Became famous for his Z-grams, special electronic messages sent directly from the CNO to expedite and improve communications with lower fleet operational elements. The messages were also known as "ZOWs" which translated into "Zumwalt's Own Words." Both Admiral Elmo Zumwalt and son (also named Elmo) served together in Vietnam, and it is thought that his son died an early death from exposure to Agent Orange as a result of that tour. A conversation with both men was documented in a PBS NewsHour broadcast in 1984, and an excerpt of the interview is available online ("In Memorium: Elmo Zumwalt" dated January 10, 2000). According to the excerpt in 1962, Admiral Zumwalt wrote a report urging the United States not to get involved with Vietnam militarily, but in 1968 he was assigned as the Commander of Naval Forces there – and was committed to winning the war. His son Elmo volunteered for riverboat duty there. To protect the sailors, who faced a 75% chance of being a casualty, Admiral Zumwalt stepped up the 3 year old campaign of spraying Agent Orange, including where his son was patrolling. Agent Orange was used to defoliate the thick forest and expose the enemy. Admiral Zumwalt said it was ironic that he had become an instrument in his own son's tragedy. The son died in 1988, at age 42. Admiral Zumwalt died January 2, 2000, at age 79. At the Admiral's funeral, President Clinton recalled that Zumwalt lived with the consequences of life's greatest loss. Thoroughgood address: Curtiss Court.

Vice Admiral John M. Poindexter – was both Deputy National Security Advisor and National Security Advisor to President Ronald Reagan from December 4, 1985 to November 25, 1986. Admiral Poindexter and his assistant, Lt Col (USMC) Oliver North are best remembered for the Iran-Contra affair which occurred during their watch. He was convicted in April 1990 of multiple felonies as a result of his actions in the Iran-Contra affair, but his convictions were reversed on appeal in 1991. Thoroughgood address: 4613 Reynolds Drive.

HISTORY OF THE THOROUGHGOOD NEIGHBORHOOD

Rear Admiral William N. Leonard – according to the Arlington National Cemetery website, Admiral Leonard was a highly decorated World War II Naval Aviator, Ace, and major player in numerous Pacific Air Battles, including a prominent part in the Battle of Midway and Coral Sea. Admiral Leonard was a founding test pilot who helped develop and improve several World War II naval airframes and weapons systems. He was believed to be the first test pilot that evaluated the capabilities and limitations of the Japanese Zero Fighter aircraft during the early stages of the war. Admiral Leonard died on August 21, 2005. Thoroughgood address: 4309 Country Club Circle.

Brigadier General Austin R. Brunelli, USMC – General Brunelli was the Thoroughgood Civic League President from 1968/69. According to an Oral History Transcript available online at the History and Museums Division, Headquarters Marine Corps, 1988, General Brunelli retired from the United States Marine Corps on July 1, 1962. In 1944 he saw action in the Kwajalein campaign, during which he earned his first (of two) Legions of Merit, and a Purple Heart. He also led battalions at Saipan and Iwo Jima. In his last tour of duty (from 1958-1962) he was assigned command of the Landing Force Training Center, Amphibious Training Command, Atlantic Fleet in Norfolk, Virginia. Thoroughgood address: 1604 Stokes Court.

Vice Admiral William Hayden Mack, USN – According to The New York Times in his obituary published January 21, 2003, Admiral Mack was the former superintendent of the Naval Academy who helped prepare the Naval Academy for the admission of women. Admiral Mack served on a destroyer that escaped the Japanese bombing of Manila harbor in World War II. He also served in the Korean and Vietnam Wars. When he retired from the Academy in 1975 he wrote 12 works of fiction, including "Captain Kilburnie" and "Pursuit of the Seawolf: A Novel of World War II." Thoroughgood address: 4232 Country Club Circle.

Rear Admiral Vernon Smith – Admiral Smith joined the Navy as a high school dropout in 1947. After eight years and seven months of enlisted service in naval aviation he attended Officer Candidate School and was commissioned in 1956. He went on to serve as Commanding Officer of five ships; Commander of an Amphibious Squadron; Commander of Naval Telecommunications, and Commander of a Naval Amphibious Group. He served as commander Amphibious Forces Sixth Fleet during the Lebanon Crisis in 1982 - 1983 and was awarded the National Order of the Cedar

WHO'S WHO

by the Lebanese Government for his service as Commander U. S. Forces Lebanon. He also served as Commander Amphibious Forces Seventh Fleet. He retired in 1989 as Vice Chief of Naval Education and Training after Forty Two Years of Naval Service. Thoroughgood address: 4125 Thoroughgood Drive.

Dr. Clarence A. (Clancy) Holland – co-founder of one of Bayside's first Family Healthcare Centers, and family physician to many residents in Thoroughgood. He was a former Virginia Beach Councilman (1970-1982), Mayor (1976-1978), and Virginia State Senator (1984-1996). Dr. Holland also had the honor of serving as the 8th King Neptune for the 1981 Virginia Beach Neptune Festival. According to the Neptune Festival website, the selection process weighs criteria such as demonstrated involvement and contribution to the quality of life in Virginia Beach, active participation in the activities of community life and an understanding of the spirit of the Neptune Festival. Thoroughgood address: 4316 Country Club Circle.

George Stenke – retired naval officer having served in World War II, Korean War, Cuban Missile Crisis, and Vietnam War. After retiring from the Navy in 1969, he established Pickett Road Enterprises, Harmony Road Properties, A-OK Moving & Storage, A-OK Mini Storage, and a wheat and soybean farm in Suffolk - a conglomerate of small companies and real estate holdings. At one time he owned Hercules Fence Company that installed fences to many of the area naval bases. For this reason his automobile license plate reads "Fences." His business success allowed Mr. Stenke to become a philanthropist. He and his (late) wife received the Bishop's Humanitarian Award from Catholic Charities of Eastern Virginia in 2006 in recognition of their years of support for Catholic Charities as well as other charities including their local parish of over 50 years, St. Pius X in Norfolk. He is the major reason St. Pius has a new parish hall (named after his wife), gym, new roof for the convent, and air conditioning throughout the Pre K-8th grade school. Another example of his generosity was in taking 300 St. Pius students to dinner and then to see the International Tattoo at Scope Convention Hall. In Thoroughgood, Mr. Stenke was instrumental in developing and improving Lake Charles and the dam that contains it. It was he and his wife that named Swan Lake Drive. And it was he who provided the initial funding advance for the publishing of this book. Thoroughgood address: 1624 Swan Lake Drive.

Gene Walters – founder and CEO of Farm Fresh Supermarket and

HISTORY OF THE THOROUGHGOOD NEIGHBORHOOD

Gene Walters' Marketplace. When he died in 2009, the Virginian Pilot (November 5, 2009) said for years Gene Walters was one of the most widely recognized faces in Hampton Roads. He was in TV commercials all the time, with a ready smile always urging customers to "tell a friend" about shopping at Farm Fresh grocery stores. Thoroughgood address: 4320 Delray Drive.

Bailey Condrey – president of Thoroughgood Civic League from 1969/70. Mr. Condrey also served in the Navy in World War II, and was the Regional Manager Chesapeake and Potomac Telephone Company (now Verizon). He was the founder of the Richmond Professional Institute (RPI) – now Virginia Commonwealth University Alumni Association. He was past chairman of the Azalea Festival, past chairman of the American Red Cross, and past president of the Norfolk Kiwanis Club. He served on the Advisory Board of Virginia Wesleyan College, former master of the Manchester Masonic Temple, and members of the Hampton Roads Chamber of Commerce, Booster Club, and Navy League. Thoroughgood address: 4237 Country Club Circle.

Bob Coffey – president of Thoroughgood Civic League 2005/06. Mr. Coffey is the retired Vice President of Sales and Industrial Development, Norfolk Southern Corporation; former Chairman of the Third Precinct Citizens' Advisory Committee; and member of the Virginia Beach Historic Sites Organizing Committee. He continues to be an avid supporter of the Adam Thoroughgood House and issues related to its improvement. He is a long-time active member of Bayside Presbyterian Church. As a decades long member of Lions International, he served as District Governor and International Counselor. Mr. Coffey was the former publisher of The Northside Tattler, owner of Travel, Inc. which used to reside in the Church Point Commons shopping center and Sage's Restaurant which used to be in the Thoroughgood Commons shopping center. Address: 4320 Delray Drive.

Mildred Alexander – renowned television talk show host during the 1970s era. Her show was on WTAR-TV (now WTKR), Channel 3 at 1:00 p.m. weekdays. Thoroughgood address: 4301 Country Club Circle.

Stanley G. Nicolay – aka "The Butterfly Man." He was born on March 14, 1917 and died December 5, 2004. He was a retired Marine Colonel aviator, and served in World War II, Korea, and Vietnam. He was a collector and expert on butterflies and insects. He (and associate Jack Clarke) shared their collection of 42,500 specimens with the Smithsonian's National Museum of Natural History. He also had an interest in orchids and bees. He wrote for National Geographic and the Journal of The Lepidopterists Society (where he was a charter member), and helped establish The Butterfly Society of Virginia in 1992. Seven butterfly species were named after Stan. He was a gifted teacher with a strong desire to share his knowledge with others, and an avid storyteller.

Starr Plimpton was a big fan of Mr. Nicolay, whom she met through her father-in-law, George Matton (past president of Thoroughgood Civic League). Mrs. Plimpton said she always thought of Stan Nicolay as the "Indiana Jones of Thoroughgood" because, like that fictional character, he possessed the true spirit of an adventurer. Outwardly, this husband, father, friend and neighbor lived a well-ordered life in the quiet Thoroughgood neighborhood. Outside of that, Mr. Nicolay traveled deep into jungle forests and scaled rock cliffs to discover new species of butterflies and orchids.

Stan Nicolay was known within the Thoroughgood neighborhood for his beekeeping. He had at least two beehives in his backyard and had other beehives in various places throughout the city. The honey that was collected from these local bees could be purchased from him. Many of the Thoroughgood residents would come by his house to get the honey from local bees because it was something that helped with allergies. Mr. Nicolay placed two beehives near the edge of the Lynnhaven River at the Adam Thoroughgood House site. This addition contributed to the historic interpretation of the importance of colonial beekeeping and how much the colonists depended on bees for honey, beeswax, and pollination of crops. He generously donated his time to maintain the hives and helped with educational bee programming whenever he was asked.

When Starr Plimpton began managing the Adam Thoroughgood House for the city, their educational programs featured making beeswax candles the way that the early colonists would have done. The cost of a block (pound) of beeswax was rather high, but Stan Nicolay brought out a box filled with large chunks of beeswax for which he refused to take any money. This generous donation was repeated on several more occasions and allowed numerous adults and children to try their hand at candle dipping and making their own beeswax candles.

Thoroughgood address: 1500 Wakefield Drive.

◄ HISTORY OF THE THOROUGHGOOD NEIGHBORHOOD

Henry Clay Hofheimer II. Although Mr. Hofheimer was not a resident in Thoroughgood, he did a lot for our neighborhood's namesake house. Henry Clay Hofheimer II is best known to Thoroughgood residents for being the president of the Adam Thoroughgood Foundation, heading the restoration efforts for the renovation of the Adam Thoroughgood House in the late 1950s, and purchasing and donating much period furniture and many artifacts for the house. But he was known in Hampton Roads for much more than that. Mr. Hofheimer was a native and life-long resident of Norfolk, and lived in the Ghent neighborhood. He was one of the region's most successful business leaders and investors. He owned Hofheimer Construction Company that built roads, bridges and airfields. He owned Southern Materials Company. He was the founder of the Hofheimer shoe chain. He was the director of the Federal Reserve Bank of Richmond. He was a leading philanthropist and community leader in the effort to advance economic development and quality of Hampton Roads in the decades after World War II. An article in the Ledger Star (January 20, 1982) said that Mr. Hofheimer was in on 95% of all the important projects in Eastern Virginia over the past 50 years. He established and developed Eastern Virginia Medical School, founded in 1973. Three U.S. Presidents honored him. He was First Citizen of Norfolk in 1958; received the Distinguished Service Award of the Virginia State Chamber of Commerce in 1964; and the Navy Distinguished Public Service Award in 1983. In 1987, the National Defense University Foundation established the Henry Clay Hofheimer Chair in Military Professionalism at the Armed Forces Staff College in Norfolk. He was on the Board of Trustees of Virginia Wesleyan College from 1964 to at least 1970 and led the drive to raise funds for the library there – hence the library is named after him. Mr. Hofheimer died February 6, 2005 at the age of 98. Amy Waters Yarsinske wrote a book on Henry Clay Hofheimer II called "Foundations and Bridges: The Life of Henry Clay Hofheimer."

G. William Whitehurst also did not live in Thoroughgood, but was a consistent presence in the neighborhood's annual potluck dinners in the 1970s and 1980s. Both he and his wife Janie were strong supporters of the Thoroughgood community for many years. He was born in Norfolk, and graduated from Maury High School in Norfolk. Congressman Whitehurst served in the U.S. House of Representatives from 1968 to 1987. After retirement, he returned to teaching at Old Dominion University.

APPENDIX A

Timeline

Thoroughgood (and nearby)	Year	Elsewhere in Virginia Beach/ Norfolk*
James Collier purchased 500 acres for original tract of Thoroughgood neighborhood; Adam Thoroughgood House (ATH) and surrounding land deeded to the ATH Foundation	1955	Ferry service from Norfolk to Portsmouth (established in 1636 by Adam Thoroughgood) discontinued
Thoroughgood Lot 299 is deeded to ATH Foundation	1956	First Boardwalk Art show held
ATH opened to public; Thoroughgood Civic League (TCL) and Thoroughgood Garden Club (TGC) formed; James Collier died	1957	I-64 crossing of the Hampton Roads Bridge Tunnel (HRBT) completed
Thoroughgood Elementary School (TES) opened	1958	Aragona Village Shopping Center opened as first shopping center in Virginia Beach (VB)
	1959	VB Council of Civic Organizations (VBCCO) founded
ATH Foundation deeded ATH and 2.29 acres to the City of Norfolk. The Garden Club of Virginia created the English garden at the ATH	1960	
Frank W. Cox High School opened at the site of original Great Neck Middle School; zoning changed Thoroughgood students from Princess Anne to Cox.	1961	Virginia Wesleyan College chartered (opened for classes in 1966); Princess Anne County Historical Society formed; Frontier City opened in VB

143

HISTORY OF THE THOROUGHGOOD NEIGHBORHOOD

	1962	Ash Wednesday Storm hit; VB Beacon began; Norfolk Division of the College of William and Mary changed its name to Old Dominion College; Frank Dusch named mayor of the future City of VB; Last passenger train enters Union Station in downtown Norfolk – 50-year-old station is officially closed
Bayside Presbyterian Church ground breaking ceremonies held for its current location (corner of Independence and Ewell)	1963	Princess Anne County is merged with the Town of VB to form City of VB
	1964	Chesapeake Bay Bridge Tunnel opened; farming ranks with tourism as a top industry in VB; VB beaches integrated; Frontier City closed
Old Donation Center (ODC) built	1965	VB General Hospital opened
ATH is listed on the National Register of Historic Places; Hermitage Garden Club formed; Bayside Area Library opened	1966	Pembroke Mall opened
Beacon article on the Thoroughgood neighborhood; City of VB completed effort to bring city water to the first section of Thoroughgood	1967	The VB-Norfolk Expressway (I-264) opened to traffic; first McDonald's Restaurant opened in VB
	1968	
ATH listed on the Virginia Landmarks Register; Haygood Shopping Center ground breaking held; court case involving zoning for entrance to Thoroughgood began	1969	E. E. Brickell integrated VB schools

TIMELINE

Low "Thoroughgood" brick wall constructed at Independence and Ewell; Cub Scout Pack 364 chartered by Bayside Presbyterian Church	1970	
	1971	VB Arts Center established
	1972	
Opened Thoroughgood entrance at Wakefield Dr; Bayside Hospital opened	1973	The first Neptune Festival held
Independence Junior High School opened; stoplight at Independence and Ewell installed	1974	VB voters upheld Sunday "Blue-law" by referendum; Mt. Trashmore opened
	1975	Bayside Hospital opened
Louise Hooper Ewell and Hazeltine Nixon died	1976	2nd crossing of the HRBT completed/tolls removed; VB Farmers Market opened
	1977	
Improvement to Pleasure House Rd announced – widening from 2 to 4 lanes; Bayville Park developed	1978	VB voters once again upheld Sunday "Blue-law" by referendum
True Value Home Center (aka Taylor Do-It Center) opened; city began construction of sewage system in Thoroughgood	1979	City Council draws "Green Line" to maintain VB's rural south
McDonald Garden Center opened; low "Thoroughgood" brick wall constructed at Independence and Five Forks	1980	Lynnhaven Mall opened; VB Convention Center (i.e., Pavilion) opened
Sewage system completed in Thoroughgood	1981	Dr. Clancy Holland served as 8th King Neptune
TCL incorporated	1982	Haygood United Methodist Church's 150th Anniversary celebrated
Egret issue at front entrance; Cox High School moved to Shorehaven Dr	1983	Columbus Center at Pembroke built; Pungo Festival began

145

HISTORY OF THE THOROUGHGOOD NEIGHBORHOOD

Ownership of left and right of Thoroughgood Sq transferred to TCL	**1984**	Southside and Peninsula merged to form "Hampton Roads"
	1985	Hurricane Gloria hit
	1986	Oystering banned from Lynnhaven River; Virginia Marine Science Museum opened; HOV lane opened on VB-Norfolk Expressway; tolls removed from the Norfolk-Portsmouth tunnels.
	1987	Dedication ceremonies held for the widening of VB Blvd from Witchduck Rd east to Rosemont Rd
	1988	Central Library opened; Meyera Oberndorf elected Mayor
	1989	Start of Church Point development; VB Center for the Arts opened; Greekfest Riots occurred; Hugh Mongus (plastic gorilla at Ocean Breeze Park) removed after being damaged by fire
Virginia Independent Automobile Dealers Association (VIADA) moved into the old Thoroughgood sales office; Parish Rd tie-in controversy; gym added to TES	**1990**	
Last TCL annual dinner dance held	**1991**	
Bayside Recreation Center opened; first Church Point Home-A-Rama held; planning began for Bayville Golf Course; last TCL potluck dinner held	**1992**	

TIMELINE

Natural gas brought to Thoroughgood (Phase 1); Thoroughgood/Church Point Commons under development; Bayside Post Office moved to Thoroughgood Rd; additional parking added to TES	1993	Catholic High School opened in VB on Princess Anne Rd (moving from former Granby St location)
Natural gas brought to Thoroughgood (Phase 2); renovation starts on TES	1994	
	1995	Seashore State Park renamed First Landing; 25-cent toll removed from the VB/Norfolk Expressway
	1996	VB Amphitheater opened; construction of the 76-mile long Lake Gaston pipeline began; Bayville Golf Club opened; Hugh Mongus returned to Ocean Breeze Park
	1997	Lake Gaston pipeline began service
Neighborhood profile in Beacon; ODC re-designated a gifted school	1998	
	1999	
	2000	Ground broken for Town Center at Pembroke
Thoroughgood high school students re-zoned from Cox to Princess Anne	2001	
	2002	Bayside Pharmacy closed
VB acquired ATH from Norfolk; Bailey Condrey (TCL President 1969-70) died	2003	VB 40th Anniversary (1963-2003); city decals for autos eliminated; VB hosted trial of Beltway Sniper
Thoroughgood residents visit Adam Thoroughgood's birthplace – Grimston, England	2004	

HISTORY OF THE THOROUGHGOOD NEIGHBORHOOD

Begin building Blackthorne Ct; new building dedicated for Bayside Library	2005	VB Convention Center opened; King Neptune statue dedicated
Deal between land owner and city to expand the grounds of the ATH	2006	
Friends of ATH formed; Reverend Howard from Grimston, England visits	2007	400th Anniversary of the first English settlement at Jamestown
TES celebrated 50th Anniversary	2008	
TCL website developed; Douglas S. Murray (TCL President 1961/62) died	2009	
	2010	
L. Charles Burlage (TCL President 1957/59) died; Kay Collier died; English elm trees at ATH cut down; ATH re-opened from renovations	2011	
Joe Ficarra (TCL President 2012/13) died	2012	Old Donation Church's 375th Anniversary celebrated; Amtrak resumes passenger train service on December 12th to Norfolk with a platform station located near Harbor Park, ending a 50-year gap in passenger rail service to Norfolk
This book was published; Don Cannell (TCL President 2000/01) died	2013	VB 50th Anniversary (1963-2013)

*Note: most of the events posted in "Elsewhere in Virginia Beach/Norfolk" came from the booklet "1607 – 2007: 400 Facts About Princess Anne County and Virginia Beach History." A few facts were gleaned from Stephen S. Mansfield's book "Princess Anne County and Virginia Beach, a pictorial history." Some facts came from the Chronology of Norfolk – available on the Kirn Memorial Library website at the Sergeant Memorial Room/Local History and Genealogical Collection. Some facts came from the "This Week in History" column in the Sunday Virginian Pilot.

APPENDIX B

Former TCL Presidents

1957-59, L. Charles Burlage

- 2706 (or 1636) Wakefield Drive, spouse: Beverly
- Our first Civic League President. See more about Mr. Burlage in Chapter 8.

1959-60, William H. Hiett

- 2717 (or 4329) Two Woods Road, spouse: Wilhelmina

1960-61, William C. Colleran, Jr.

- 2704 (or 4312) Westwell Lane, spouse: (first wife) Shirley C., (second wife) Martha M.
- Army veteran and in 79th Division during World War II, died June 12, 2011 at Sentara Bayside Hospital. He was an accountant.

1961-62, Douglas S. Murray, Lt Commander, SC, USN

- 2710 (or 1628) Wakefield Drive, spouse: Beamie, and the 1959 Thoroughgood Civic League Directory shows him at 2717 Thoroughgood Drive
- Graduated from Harvard Business School; served in the Navy as a Supply Officer in World War II, Korean, and Vietnam wars. Retired from Naval service in 1969, and went on to become the Director of Finance and Administration and Treasurer of the Virginia Port Authority. He served as an elder at Bayside Presbyterian Church, and he and his wife were active in the boy/girl scouts. He was a

◄ HISTORY OF THE THOROUGHGOOD NEIGHBORHOOD

Board member on the Virginia Beach SPCA, and president of Douglas Realty Corporation. He built and operated the Coral Isle Motel Apartments in Norfolk, and owned the gulf-stream fishing boat "Chivas Regal" in Hatteras Island. He and spouse Beamie were married for almost 65 years. He died April 2012.

1962-63, Elwood E. Braunbeck, Sr.

- 2728 Two Woods Road, spouse: Ruby
- Associated with Braunbeck's Moving and Storage

1963-64, Lyman H. Stone, Jr.

- 2700 Westwell Lane, spouse: Naida

1964-65, B. R. (Beverly Randolph) Middleton

- 2718 (or 1612) Wakefield Drive, spouse: Ann, Ernestine
- See Chapter 8 for B. R. Middleton's many civic leadership roles
- Died July 12, 1996

1965-66, J. Willoughby Butt

- 1500 Whitethorne Road, spouse: Margaret

1966-67, Albert S. Harden, Jr.

- 4332 Thoroughgood Drive, spouse: Selma
- Quoted in the Beacon's article on the Thoroughgood neighborhood on May 18, 1967. He said in the article that the main goals of the Civic League during his presidency were to get city water and city sewer for residents. The Civic League was also still actively pursuing establishment of a swim and country club on Country Club Circle during this time.
- Worked to take over deed restrictions, but Thorogood Corporation did not give authority during his tenure.

1967-68, William J. Manning, Captain, USN

- 1621 Westerfield Road, spouse: Betsy
- Presided during the time period where city water was brought to Thoroughgood.

FORMER TCL PRESIDENTS

- Civic League Constitution and Bylaws were updated: "Bayside Road" was changed to Independence Boulevard. Also this version is the first seen in Civic League records to include Thoroughgood Estates – identified as "that portion of the Frizzell Farm bounded north of Independence Boulevard and west of Ewell Road."

1968-69, Austin R. Brunelli, Brig. General (retired USMC)

- 1604 Stokes Court, spouse: Bernie
- Presided over the start (and bulk) of the 14-year controversy over the front entrance to Thoroughgood
- See Chapter 8 for more on General Brunelli

1969-70, Bailey L. Condrey

- 4237 Country Club Circle, spouse: Sally
- Presided over the continuation of the 14 year controversy over the Front Entrance to Thoroughgood
- See Chapter 8 for Bailey Condrey's accomplishments outside of Thoroughgood
- Died April 29, 2003

1970-71, Richard L. Lindell

- 2819 (or 4113) Thoroughgood Drive, spouse: Gay
- Presided during the time Thoroughgood Garden Club constructed the low brick wall at Ewell Road and Independence Boulevard

1971-72, Roy M. Sudduth, Captain

- 1637 Arrowhead Point, spouse: Shirley
- Shirley Sudduth passed away of December 28, 2012. According to her obituary in the Virginian Pilot (December 30, 2012), Roy Sudduth passed away in 1983. After his passing, Shirley Sudduth sold her Thoroughgood home and moved to the Great Neck area

1972-73, W. George Matton, Jr., Captain

- 19 (or 4112) Hermitage Point, spouse: Nevett
- Presided over the early fight to control the Thoroughgood Colony development, during the cut-through of Wakefield Drive to Independence Boulevard, and the battle to oppose zoning the front

HISTORY OF THE THOROUGHGOOD NEIGHBORHOOD

entrance from commercial to O-1 (office) as a part of the new zoning ordinance for Virginia Beach, and Bayside Development Plan.

1973-74, Knox R. Burchett

- 1412 Dunstan Lane, spouse: Mickey
- Mickey Burchett is a member of Suburban Women's Club

1974-75, Henry O. Pezzela

- 4704 Thoroughgood Drive, spouse: Peggy
- Instrumental in City Council advancing the Thoroughgood community to top of the priority list for water and sewage installation. That was done by urging residents to commit to immediate hook-up once lines were available, thereby ensuring quick city revenue from such action.
- Stopped the threat of a major business development at the front main entrance by large resident turnout at City Council hearings, which resulted in Council rejection of requesting zoning change.
- Presided over an issue to retain a city ordnance concerning the parking of major recreational vehicles and boats in front of houses. The city voted 6 to 5 in 1975 to continue the ordnance where no major recreational vehicles may be parked on any public street or right-of-way for more than three hours and must be stored inside or behind a residence.
- Peggy Pezella is a member of the Suburban Woman's Club and Hermitage Garden Club. She was past president of Sentara Virginia Beach General Auxiliary and a Virginia Symphony Trustee.

1975-76, Charles D. "Spider" Webb, Captain, USN (retired)

- 1609 Allerson Lane, spouse: Lucine
- Presided during time of Civic League opposition to the proposed rezoning of area of Wakefield at Independence to townhouses (Thoroughgood Colony)
- Died August 1996

1976-77, Harold T. Mahler

- 4517 Biscayne Drive, spouse: Midge
- Presided the year the Civic League began maintaining the front entrance – asked each family to contribute $3.00 each to offset the cost

FORMER TCL PRESIDENTS

1977-78, Alexander L. Redon, Captain, USN (retired)

- 4158 Hermitage Road, spouse: Royana
- Presided during Civic League opposition to proposed rezoning of the northeast intersection of Dunstan Lane/Wakefield Drive (from R-1 to R-3)

1978-79, John E. Reed

- 4645 Reynolds Drive, spouse: Peggy
- Presided over establishment of the Thoroughgood Watch Program, over the installation of sewers in Thoroughgood, and during the time Pleasure House Road was widened

1979-80, Robert G. Krebs, Colonel

- 1529 Adam Road, spouse: Janis
- Dealt with problems of sewer installation, the introduction of the Block Mothers Program; and dealt with continued opposition to the proposed rezoning of the northeast section of Dunstan Lane and Wakefield Drive

1980-81, Ernestine K. Middleton

- 1612 Wakefield Drive, spouse: (the late) B. R.
- Frist female president of Thoroughgood Civic League
- Presidency dealt with problems of sewer installation, the initiation of the Block Security program, and the proposed Comprehensive Bikeway Plan for Virginia Beach (as it pertained to Five Forks Road)
- See Chapter 8 for more of Mrs. Middleton's many civic leadership roles

1981-82, John E. Cousins, Captain, USN

- 4160 Hermitage Road, spouse: Marcia
- Passed away April 14, 2010 in Naples, Florida (survived by spouse Marcia)

1982-83, John M. "Jack" Barry, Commander, USN

- 1613 Five Forks Road, spouse: Joyce
- Presided when Thoroughgood Civic League was incorporated; early efforts to re-zone the property that would eventually become

HISTORY OF THE THOROUGHGOOD NEIGHBORHOOD

Blackthorne Court; and the start of the "egret" and townhouse issues at the front entrance.

- Mr. Barry joined the Navy becoming a Naval Aviator in 1955. In his first squadron he flew seaplanes. Two interesting tours of duty were in Panama and Bermuda. In a later Squadron, he flew the new P3 Orion. An avid tennis player, Mr. Barry played as tennis doubles partner with George H. W. Bush at the first annual convention of the Association of Naval Aviation in 1976. When he retired from active duty he initially flew for Eastern Airlines. At the start of the Vietnam War there was a shortage of pilots, Mr. Barry returned to the Navy, becoming an active duty officer and finally retired in 1980 with 30 year's service. Upon retirement, he worked as Operations Manager for the Norfolk Chamber of Commerce for five years where part of his position was as director of the Azalea Festival. Daughter Liane served as an attendant for a NATO princess. He later worked for DePaul Hospital as Vice President of Marketing and Development and then retired. Mr. Barry served as the 4th president of the Hampton Roads Naval Museum Foundation, which was founded about 1984 to support the Naval Museum in Pennsylvania House aboard the US Naval Station, Norfolk. This Foundation pledged to the city of Norfolk a half million dollars in support of the building of the Nauticus Museum. Mr. Barry was on the vestry of Old Donation Episcopal Church. He was the president of the Hampton Roads Council of the Navy League of the United States, where he took a small Council and revitalized it with interesting state, local and military speakers. This greatly increased attendance, setting the stage for what has become a large, robust local council today. He has been state and regional presidents, and finally a national director. Mr. Barry is currently National Director, emeritus and entered in the Navy League Hall of Fame.
- Mrs. Barry joined Thoroughgood Garden Club in 1967 and Hermitage Garden Club in 1975. She is also a twenty-two year member of Suburban Woman's Club and Council of Garden Clubs in Virginia Beach. She has held numerous offices in all the clubs including president of TGC in 1979-1981, and has been the treasurer and photographer for all four clubs, in addition to being the photographer for Old Donation Episcopal Church.

FORMER TCL PRESIDENTS

1983-84, Maurice "Mike" F. Conner

- 4344 Two Woods Road, spouse: Gloria
- Presided over the conclusion of the front entrance issues (egrets, townhouses), including his picture in the newspaper in front of the Thoroughgood entrance as it appeared in 1983/84

1984-85, Peggy Moore

- 1632 Whitethorne Road, spouse: Robert
- Worked for ODU in the Office of Planning and Budget; part owner of Lielin, Goldsmiths, Designers, Crafters of Fine Jewelry
- Presided over the receipt of the deed of easement at Thoroughgood Square to the Thoroughgood Civic League, and follow-on issue to beautify the entrance within strict timeframes

1985-86, James L. Guion, Jr., Lt. Colonel

- 4220 Hermitage Road, spouse: Annette
- Continued dealing with the issue of front entrance beautification post Thoroughgood Square deed easement
- Second Vice President and Program Chairman in 1987 of the Virginia Beach Council of Civic Leagues. Most notable of his programs was "Will We Trash Virginia," a presentation by Dr. Jacquelin T. Robertson, Dean of the School of Architecture at the University of Virginia. The theme was that poor planning and development would be costly and bad for Virginia. The meeting was well attended filling the City Council Chamber with some having to stand.
- Annette Guion was the president of Thoroughgood Garden Club in 1983-85 and again in 1999-2001

1986-87, Leonard L. Tucker, Jr., Commander, USN

- 2403 (or 4645) Thoroughgood Drive, spouse: Marty
- Parents lived next door (4641 Thoroughgood Drive), and father (Leonard L. Tucker, Sr.) had long ties with Thoroughgood Civic League as its Treasurer
- Died February 18, 2005 in Englewood, Florida (reported in the Daily Press in an article, February 20, 2005)

HISTORY OF THE THOROUGHGOOD NEIGHBORHOOD

1987-88, Curtis R. Catron

- 1600 Arrowhead Court, spouse: Nancy
- Associated with Catron Insurance Agency
- Presided when the Five Forks "paper" Road was closed – i.e., where the road crossed the old Bayville Farms (i.e., Church Point neighborhood), and the start of plans for the Church Point development

1988-89, Terri Dennis

- 1360 Wakefield Circle, spouse: David
- Presided over the start of the Church Point/Parish Road tie-in issue, and the continuation of the Church Point neighborhood development
- Executive Vice President of Tidewater Coffee Distributors, Ltd.

1989-90, Dr. James F. Reske, DDS

- 4121 Thoroughgood Drive, spouse: Gayle
- Presided over the closure of the Church Point/Parish Road tie-in issue, and continuation of the Church Point neighborhood development

1990-91, Patrick F. Harney, Commander

- 1408 Rust Drive, and 1428 Sir Richard Road, spouse: Ann
- Presided when the Virginia Independent Automobile Dealers Association moved into the old sales office at the end of Thoroughgood Square

1991-92, John R. Akers, Captain, SC, USN (retired)

- 4132 Country Club Circle, spouse: Carolyn
- Presided over the issue of a bike path from Church Point to Parish Road

1992-93 and 1993-94, Stephen J. Matton

- 1505 Westerfield Road, spouse: Starr
- Presided over the start of the Bayville Golf Course Water Issue; the construction of Church Point Commons and the issue of ingress/egress through Thoroughgood Square; and bringing natural gas into the homes in Thoroughgood

FORMER TCL PRESIDENTS

1994-95, Kent J. ("Curly") Weber, Commander

- 1508 Adam Road, spouse: Mary
- Presided over the continuation of the Bayville Golf Course Water Issue; the construction of Thoroughgood Commons; and the creation of the Neighborhood Watch program

1995-96, Nancy Koch

- Initially at 4725 Newgate Court, 1457 Ewell Road, 1405 Dunstan Circle, spouse: Richard J., Jr.
- A real estate expert for the Thoroughgood area, and quoted in an article in Virginia Beach Living (dated 5/26/2005) regarding the Blackthorne Court development in Thoroughgood
- Presided over the conclusion of the Bayville Golf Course Water Issue
- Past president of Thoroughgood Elementary School PTA

1996-97, Clyde V. March, Jr., Lt Colonel, USAF (retired)

- 4621 Thoroughgood Drive, spouse: Gail
- Dealt with drainage issues in Thoroughgood after severe rain storms struck the area
- Pursued restitution when a motor vehicle accident damaged the low brick wall at the entrance of Independence and Five Forks
- Very active in maintaining property values in Thoroughgood
- Spearheaded the establishment and continuation of the Neighborhood Watch Program
- Requested the city install "No Parking" signs on Thoroughgood Square
- Assisted with the development of this historical account of the Thoroughgood neighborhood
- Gail March is a long-standing member of the Thoroughgood Garden Club since 1993, and member of the Suburban Woman's Club. She was recognized in The Flagship (August 16, 2012) for volunteering more than 8,000 hours of her time to the Navy-Marine Corps Relief Society's "Budget for Baby" program, which assists new or prospective parents learn about the impact a new baby can have on the financial situation of the family. Part of the volunteering was in knitting more than 237 items for the layette program. Mrs. March

HISTORY OF THE THOROUGHGOOD NEIGHBORHOOD

was awarded the 2012 NMCRS Layette Volunteer of the Year Award in April 2012.

1997-98, M. Powell Peters

- 1608 Keeling Landing Road, spouse: Jacque
- Dealt with mailbox bombings; partnered with Church Point homeowners to address dredging issues in the western channel of the Lynnhaven River; drainage/flooding issues in the neighborhood; a ground water permit modification from Bayville Golf Course; and petitioned the 3rd Police Precinct to monitor vehicle speeding in the neighborhood
- Quoted in the "At Home" article in the Virginian Pilot (dated November 14, 1998) regarding a profile of the neighborhood. Mr. Peters is a descendant of Adam Keeling, an indentured servant of Adam Thoroughgood, which is why he chose to purchase property on Keeling Landing Road.
- Attorney
- Jacque Peters has been a member of the Thoroughgood Garden Club since 1996, and was its president in 2011-2013 and is an elder at Bayside Presbyterian Church

1998-99, Ernestine K. Middleton

- 1612 Wakefield Drive, spouse: (the late) B. R.
- See Chapter 8 for Mrs. Middleton's many civic leadership roles

1999-2000, Dr. Truman D. Baxter, DDS

- 1605 Allerson Lane, spouse: Sally
- Worked to establish a program to educate Thoroughgood residents on what could or could not be done in enforcing code restrictions in the neighborhood, and to handle resident complaints

2000-01, Donald T. Cannell, Captain, USN (retired)

- 4236 Country Club Circle, spouse: Audre
- Presided over the redistricting of Thoroughgood from Frank W. Cox High School to Princess Anne High School
- Don was an active member of Bayside Presbyterian Church. He was the Church Treasurer; served nine years as an active ordained Elder;

FORMER TCL PRESIDENTS

- and was elected Elder Emeritus. Audre remains active as a co-chair of the Bayside Food Pantry serving the area's needy families.
- Don passed away June 23, 2013

2001-02, Larry LaRue, Captain, USN (retired)

- 1616 Arrowhead Point
- Started an initiative to preside over the cleanup of Lynnhaven River coves and channels in Thoroughgood and actively participated in the project in/around 2011 and continuing issues with high school redistricting.

2002-03, Kathy Williams

- 1600 Keeling Landing Road, spouse: Richard
- Wholesale flower market owner who currently supplies the greens for the Holiday Greens Sale for the Thoroughgood Garden Club, and has been a member of that club since 2000. Also a CPA, Healthcare CFO.

2003-04, Tom Forrest

- 1705 Five Forks, spouse: Jamie
- Presided during the time that the City of Norfolk transferred ownership of the Adam Thoroughgood House to the City of Virginia Beach, and during the visit of Thoroughgood residents to Grimston, England
- Management Consultant; Engineer; U. S. Naval Officer

2004-05, Norman V. Stones

- 1413 Sir Richard Road, spouse: Susan
- Presided during the time Blackthorne Court was built

2005-06, Robert W. Coffey

- 4320 Delray Drive, spouse: Anne
- Brokered the deal between the city and Robert Parise to purchase the waterfront lot adjacent and to the rear of the Adam Thoroughgood House
- Quoted in the Virginian Pilot/Hampton Roads section (July 17, 2011) regarding the controversy surrounding the Adam Thoroughgood House renovation

◄ HISTORY OF THE THOROUGHGOOD NEIGHBORHOOD

- Very active in maintaining property values in Thoroughgood
- Assisted with the development of this historical account of the Thoroughgood neighborhood
- Active member of Bayside Presbyterian Church
- See Chapter 8 for more on Mr. Coffey

2006-07, David Redmond (1st half), David C. Johnson (2nd half)

- David Redmond, Ewell Road, resigned the Presidency of Thoroughgood Civic League to accept a City Council-appointed position as the Bayside District representative on the Virginia Beach Planning Council
- David C. Johnson, 4209 Country Club Circle, spouse: Glenda. David Johnson presided during the time Reverend Howard from Grimston, England (i.e., Adam Thoroughgood's birthplace) visited Virginia Beach, and the Adam Thoroughgood House
- Glenda Johnson is a member of Thoroughgood Garden Club and is its president in 2013/2014

2007-08, Richard Stuart

- 4500 Thoroughgood Drive, spouse: Terry
- Revitalized the neighborhood picnic to the current "Patriots, Popsicles & a Picnic." The picnic used to be the 3rd Sunday in May (recall it replaced the dinner dance in the olden days of Thoroughgood) and moved to July 4th due to weather challenges in May

2008-09, David C. Johnson

- 4209 Country Club Circle, spouse: Glenda
- Changed the venue of activities to appeal to younger families
- Retired as a Lt. Colonel in the United States Marine Corps; currently an attorney with the Virginia Beach Law Group
- Glenda Johnson is a member of the Thoroughgood Garden Club, and is its president in 2013-2014

2009-10, J. Mark Atkins

- 4537 Biscayne Drive, spouse: Susan
- Presided over the creation of the Thoroughgood Neighborhood website, and the start of the "Movies on the Lawn" program

FORMER TCL PRESIDENTS

- Susan Atkins is member of the Thoroughgood Garden Club, and a six-year member of the Thoroughgood Civic League Board (Corresponding Secretary)
- Susan Atkins publishes the newsletter "Thoroughly Good News," and writes the column "Gardening Corner" in the newsletter. Under her tutelage the newsletter doubled in size, thanks in part to a broad expansion in ads sold.

2010-11, Richard Stuart

- 4500 Thoroughgood Drive, spouse: Terry
- Quoted in the Virginian Pilot/Hampton Roads section (July 17, 2011) regarding the controversy surrounding the Adam Thoroughgood House renovation
- Spearheaded effort to renovate and reinstall the "Thoroughgood" scrollwork after it had fallen from the center brick structure at the entrance to Thoroughgood in 2013

2011-12, Mark Joynt

- 4000 Thoroughgood Drive, spouse: Karen
- Presided during controversy of the group home on Ewell Road, and the controversy over the Adam Thoroughgood House renovation
- Karen Joynt is a member of Thoroughgood Garden Club, and was its president in 2009-2011.

2012-2013, Joe Ficarra, Al Lozito

- Joe: 4425 Chandler Lane, spouse: Bess
- The Ficarras were second-generation owners of Ficarra Jewelers at Haygood Shopping Center, which was founded by his father in 1944
- Mr. Ficarra was president for a short two months before he died on September 8, 2012
- Al Lozito: 4657 Curtiss Drive
- Presided during the compilation of this history of the Thoroughgood neighborhood

Note 1: Many of the Presidents held other Board posts before and after their Presidency. These posts often included much more than the traditional President-Elect and Vice President positions.

◄ HISTORY OF THE THOROUGHGOOD NEIGHBORHOOD

Note 2: House numbering appeared to have changed from the initial years in the neighborhood. For example, L. Charles Burlage initially was listed as living at 2706 Wakefield Drive. Today, there is no such number on that street. Later records show him living at 1636 Wakefield Drive. The change was perhaps related to the general change of address from "Bayside, Virginia" to "Virginia Beach, Virginia" when the town of Virginia Beach merged with Princess Anne County.

Note 3: Addresses, military ranks (as applicable), spouses, etc. were gleaned from Civic League records – taken usually from the time of the person's presidency. They may not represent current or complete data.

APPENDIX C

Membership/Dues Trends

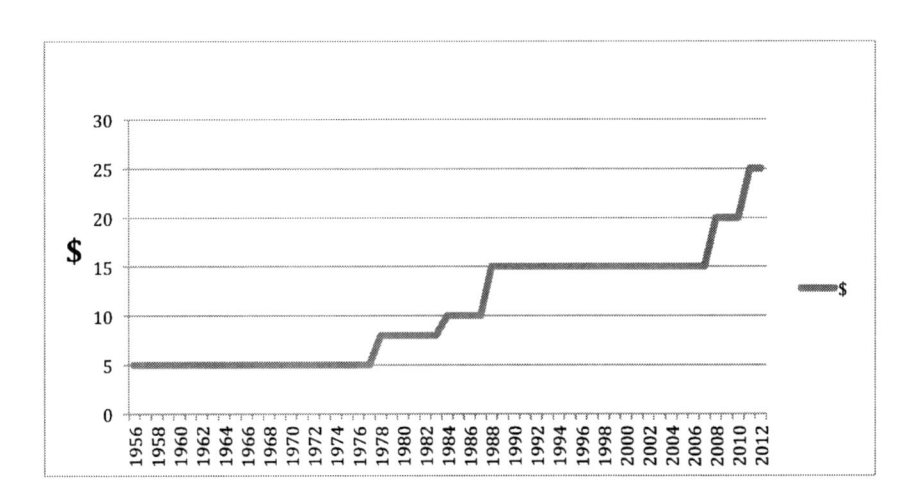

For those interested in tracking trends – membership dues for the Thoroughgood Civic League have remained relatively low over the years. The first 20 years of our neighborhood's existence (1957-1977) dues were $5 per year. In 1978-1983 dues increased to $5 annually plus a voluntary donation of an additional $3 to go towards the newly acquired front gate maintenance. From 1984-1987 dues were $10 per year. For the period 1988-2007, dues were $15 per year. In 2008-2010, dues increased to $20 a year, and in 2011-2012 annual dues are at the current rate of $25 per year. The number of paid memberships in 2011/2012 was approximately 370 families.

◄ HISTORY OF THE THOROUGHGOOD NEIGHBORHOOD

What does this assessment buy? According to the audit of treasury records for fiscal year 2011/2012, the major expenses were maintenance costs of $2,938. This included refurbishing/rebuilding the four large front gate light fixtures, and fabrication of new signs used to announce the events throughout the year. In addition, $2,764 was spent on expenses related to those events (i.e. movie night, picnic, 4th of July Parade, and Easter Egg Hunt). Distribution of the newsletter cost $2,345; lawn service at the front entrance cost $2,100; compilation and distribution of the directory cost $1,550; and utilities for the front entrance was $185.